# BOLTERS AND COOLERS

# BOLTERS AND COOLERS

## *Tales of a Bouncer, Bodyguard and Cook*

*Noel Watson*

**BALBOA.**
PRESS
A DIVISION OF HAY HOUSE

ISBN: 978-1-4525-5630-7 (sc)
ISBN: 978-1-4525-5631-4 (hc)
ISBN: 978-1-4525-5629-1 (e)

Library of Congress Control Number: 2012914148

Balboa Press books may be ordered through booksellers or by contacting:

Balboa Press
A Division of Hay House
1663 Liberty Drive
Bloomington, IN 47403
www.balboapress.com
1-(877) 407-4847

Because of the dynamic nature of the Internet, any web addresses or links contained in this book may have changed since publication and may no longer be valid. The views expressed in this work are solely those of the author and do not necessarily reflect the views of the publisher, and the publisher hereby disclaims any responsibility for them.

The author of this book does not dispense medical advice or prescribe the use of any technique as a form of treatment for physical, emotional, or medical problems without the advice of a physician, either directly or indirectly. The intent of the author is only to offer information of a general nature to help you in your quest for emotional and spiritual well-being. In the event you use any of the information in this book for yourself, which is your constitutional right, the author and the publisher assume no responsibility for your actions.

Any people depicted in stock imagery provided by Thinkstock are models, and such images are being used for illustrative purposes only.
Certain stock imagery © Thinkstock.

Printed in the United States of America

Balboa Press rev. date: 8/13/2012

To Tina, the chosen one for your enlightenment
and support on this journey

"Too many people in rock and roll think about living fast and dying young"

"Music's like anything. It's like wine, like martial arts—everyone thinks when you become a black belt you've made it, but black belt means you've learnt the basics"

---Jimmy Barnes

*Do or Die*

# Contents

# PREFACE

Only a fool suffers the 5 second stare down or the sharp end of the sword. Many moons ago I've been told I have a unique story to tell which all began when my American brother-in-law suggested I write a cook book for hard-men. I wanted to give people an all access pass to the in's and out of working doors and a rare glimpse at Australia's hard man of Rock and Roll. I've been intrigued by Martial Arts Academy, Zen Do Kai which means 'the best of everything in progression.' Soke Bob Jones, the founder, promoted the style using an open system which I liked due to the practicality. Zen Do Kai embraces the many ideas from around the world which allows influences, techniques and practices used in Thai Kickboxing. This is what set it apart from other more traditional forms of Karate.

In the 70's from street fighting to security, working doors was like crowd control without a badge. I felt compelled to tell the security side of the equation, especially at a time when there were no mobile phones or security cameras.

During the 1990's violence in pubs and clubs became a major public concern, a study showed over 100 incidents of aggression within a 2 hour period in 36 out of 45 venues in Sydney, Australia.

As head security for Australian Rock Singer, Jimmy Barnes I also wanted to give people a look at life on the road and what went on outside the main arena. This is my voice and although I am no angel, there are three sides to the story; right, wrong and the truth.

Thank you to my wife and partner for helping me co-write this book and for the hours it took to translate action into words. A big thank you to my brother-in-law, Micheal Markrich for all your dedication and support in launching 'Street fighter in the Kitchen', your encouragement has allowed me to pursue the completion of this project. To Rod, for without you these stories would not be possible. To Jimmy, you are one hell of a mate, thank you for teaching me the ability to keep on going and for Jane the opportunities you have given me.

To Soke Bob Jones, your wisdom is embedded in me for life. To all the Zen Do Kai Boys(too many to mention) especially the first generation, O'Kaicho Malcolm Anderson, Paul, Gary and Trevor Pettersen, Steve Fyfield, Gordon Mitchell, Noel Rush, Tony Quinn, Nicky O'Callahan, Wayne Ogden, Shaun and Terry Keating. To all the Red Hill Boys, where ever you may be, Eddie Whitnell, Coffin Cheaters and the Odin's Warriors. To all of our Friends and Supporters who became part of the Hulala Ohana, a very big Mahalo to Phil, Kathleen and my extended family in Hawaii for really teaching me the art of Aloha and giving. To Mikayla Markrich, for your case study on Hulala. To my Mum and Dad for sticking by me through thick and thin and savoury mince. Thank you to Brian Setzer, Slim Jim and Lee Rocker of the Stray Cats, Swannie(John Swan) and all the band and crew that I worked with.

In memory of my dad Morris Watson,father-in-law Primo Racuya, Ron Smart, Julian Kovacs, Big Noel Hatwell, Micheal Hutchence and Genghis

*Noel's tile breaking punch*

CHAPTER 1

# Bolters, Coolers and Cooks

## Bolters

The first Australian bushrangers were escaped convicts called *Bolters.* These early settlers were the worst criminals sent to Tasmania, known as Van Diemen's Land which was colonised by the British in 1803 as a penal colony. They hid in the bush from the police and survived by robbing banks and stealing from settlers and rich squatters. These men bolted to defy authority and run away from the harsh conditions and treatment that they received as convicts. Others were just looking for adventure and boredom from everyday work. Some were as young as fifteen years old. In the gold digging years of 1860's the bushrangers were freeborn, young men with a wild or vicious streak. Their exploits were spectacular and they won a kind of fame, but mostly died by the gun or gallows.

## Coolers

A Bouncer also known as Doorman or *Cooler* is an informal term for a type of security guard employed at venues such as bars, nightclubs or concerts. Professional Coolers mainly check legal age, refuse entry for aggressive behavior, intoxication or non-compliance with statutory or establishment rules. Bouncers are often required where crowd size, clientele or alcohol consumption may make arguments or fights a possibility. In the 1870's they were used in high-class brothels to prevent patrons from roughing up the girls or evading payment. The 'protective presence' of the bouncers was one of the reasons the girls considered themselves superior to lower class freelancers. These professional coolers were also referred to as 'chucker outs.'

This is a story about a modern day Bolter and Cooler who wanted to escape the guts of the city and defy the harsh conditions of everyday street life. He became a martial artist hoping he could heal the scars of street life and search for an easier way to make a living. Although, he becomes the master in martial arts and completes the full circle he realizes he becomes the student of life. Through his journey in this violent way of life, he unknowingly searches for a way to be a more conscious human being whilst living in an unconscious environment.

## Sunday night at Gobbles

Most of the people who came into Hulala Cafe in Byron Bay and saw me standing at the grill serving fish tacos, duck spring rolls and goat cheese wontons didn't know that I hadn't always done this for a living. They just saw a bloke doing several things at once turning Kal-bi beef sticks, cutting quesadillas and enchiladas or putting together the "Hulala Pupu Platter" stopping from time to time to mix more *misoyaki* sauce(miso, shoyu and beer) or *huli-huli* sauce( Hawaiian barbecue sauce made from tomato sauce, pineapple and brown sugar). If they had looked closely they would have seen that I always stood on the balls of my feet and subconsciously in a karate stance. Whatever I was doing my eyes never wandered far from the food on the grill. Once or twice people came up and asked me where I learned to cook. I nodded and smiled and never answered. I never told them that I learned the art of cooking through martial arts or that part of my preparation for running my own cafe had come from being a doorman in some of the roughest clubs in Western Australia. In my world I didn't know any chefs or foodies I knew bodyguards, rock and roll bands, bikers and part-time gangsters.

It takes a certain person to be a doorman. You have to be able to stand up for 12 hours or more while being confronted by all walks of life. You can be spat upon, verbally abused, hit with objects like rocks, knives, bottles, baseball bats, and sometimes even cars. Most seasoned doorman can never live a normal life because of what they have seen or heard. Some sleep all day, and only feel comfortable socializing with their own kind. You have to think is it really worth it when nine times out of 10 you will be found guilty if taken to court because of your already tainted police docket. The case could be as simple as refusing entry to a law clerk and then he can make your life hell on court day. Anything can happen. Your health and fighting ability starts to fade and that is normally when shit hits the fan in the wee hours of the morning. That's why if somebody asks you outside in this day and age Don't GO! It is no longer a bad boxing match and nearly always can end in a tragic way. An awkward punch, the other fellows head hits the pavement and then that's a lethal contact. Take a leaf out of my book; nobody wants to be in that situation 20 years jail for what, he called me a dirty rat. It takes a bigger man to walk away, talk to any seasoned fighter and he'll tell you it's not worth it. If you want to be a good doorman there are a few basic rules you should know. Take three deep breaths before you make a decision. Keep your level of fitness strong, always have good posture, use focus and discipline, have good communication skills. And in extreme situations disregard all of that and make sure you can fight like hell.

But you are what you are. I never planned to leave the security lifestyle and go into cooking. During the 1980's I was working with bands like Cold Chisel which was then one of Australia's premier rock and roll bands. In 1983 Jimmy Barnes left the band to go on his own and asked me to do his security. As Jimmy's bodyguard –cum—karate trainer there weren't many places we didn't go together. He was touring with ZZ Top at the time as the opening act and I went with him on his American tour. He had a special nickname for me 'Mo Fo'. It was a much better name than 'Crazy Noel', the nickname that had followed me like a plaque since I started training in 'Zen Do Kai' with 'Soke' Bob Jones.

As a 6th degree black belt we toured in New York, London, Tokyo and to practically every country town and capital city in Australia and New Zealand. Being a cook in a restaurant was the farthest thing from my mind. Those were the days of an amazing race; airport check-ins, excess baggage, hotel lobbies, eating $25 hamburgers at the Waldorf Astoria while making sure Jimmy and his family were safe. Every six months or so the tour would come to a grinding halt, Jimmy would take a break and I would return to help my mate, Rod Stroud in the security business. Gobbles was an average venue with black painted walls, loud music and aggressive drunks. These were not places for the faint hearted. It was a good life for about ten years. I would work the tour, make some money, unwind and then work the nightclubs with Rod and the Zen Do Kai boys. However, there was never a time to actually unwind.

When you are a doorman you live off your reputation, the beauty marks or scars and bruises you have on your face are part of the job. Since I am no longer a doorman I can tell you some of mine. I've had three head blows from Crown Lager bottles each one of them exploding. One from a soccer hooligan which was refused entry, one from a brawl which erupted in the bar and the other inside the kebab shop while on tour with the Stray Cats. At an open air gig held at the Melbourne Music Bowl, someone used a .50 cent piece in a slingshot; hit my chest (through my leather jacket) which tore a huge chunk of skin and left a three inch scar. I've had numerous broken noses, rocks thrown at me, stitches on my eyes and the ultimate 'double black eye'. That's when you get a black eye and get into another fight before that black eye heals. I've managed the usual broken knuckles and a few minor grazes from dodging cars. It is all in a day's work. But after a while if you're smart you learn a few techniques that lessen the need for fights. For example, if drunks are just obnoxious it was easy enough to say, "excuse me but you have won a special prize from the bar, come through this door please." I would open a door to the outside and lock it behind them when they stepped through. You weren't working with geniuses. In fact it worked every time. There are two things I always recommend that people never do. If you get thrown out of a club by a doorman, it's not a good idea to come back later with friends hoping to even the score. Doormen are trained to fight for keeps. They are used to hurting people and getting hurt. The second thing is never pinch a bar maid's bum. Yes they are usually good looking but they may also be someone else's girlfriend. I have seen doormen throw guys through glass windows especially if it is their girlfriend. But few of these problems occur on a regular basis and I was used to the lifestyle. It was a job that put cash in my pocket, allowed me to work with my own kind and besides I didn't know any better. Then one Sunday night everything changed. I was working at Gobbles with four other guys backing me up when all of a sudden the big black front door swung open and 3 Pacific Islanders, pushed back the rope and left for the night. Each over 6 feet tall, broad shouldered, big fuzzy hair and weighing 20 stone. I watched them leave and head towards the parking lot. One of them happened to have a tin of beer in their hand. I didn't think more about it. The footsteps of their heavy boots could be heard on the pavement as they walked away from the club in the street. I watched them go and thought how quiet the night had turned out to be. Then from behind me I hear in a strong Australian accent.

"Hey you! you can't take beer off the premises." Technically he was right. The WA Liquor and Gaming Commission are clear that you are not supposed to leave clubs with open containers of alcohol. But I wasn't working for them. They were out of the club and almost into their car.

"Let it go", I said to Laurie with a wave of my hand. "It's only a half can of beer." Now it's just before closing. But Laurie still won't let it go. Then as I am standing there wondering what the hell he was doing he steps forward and shouts loudly into the night. "You heard what I said! Bring it back!" Now in more than ten years in security at big rock concerts and being in big fights in country towns with crazy drunks I had learned that there were some things in this business that were smart to do and some things that are not. There are times to be a samurai and times to keep your mouth shut. Apparently, they thought so too. I watched in slow motion as they suddenly stopped, they turned around with anger in their eyes. I signalled Dean and the other doorman to push the automatic button which would light up a warning system to the rest of the doorman upstairs. Green indicated to approach with observation, yellow was to proceed with caution as situation may be verbal within a larger group, and red meant physical and extreme situation. I took one look at their mouths, frothing doing a washing machine cycle. I knew they were on something, ecstasy, speed or a combination that would make them even stronger and full of confidence. "Laurie! I told you not to worry about it!" As they approached, I knew it wasn't going to be a friendly chat. I put my hand on my chin to guard my head in case they start to swing wildly. My peripheral vision was panoramic; I began *sussing* (analysing) them out to see if they were tooled up. I always do a 5 second appraisal. Then I thought I'm sick of making excuses for guys who are pissed with bad manners. Bring it on! "C'mon Guys," I said in a friendly conversational way, "It's over a half can of beer, forget about it." I stepped back as a non-threatening gesture just enough to let them try and read me. "Aww...FUCK off!" the biggest one said. Oh well, guess he didn't read right, so I set the bait and let him come close to me. Always at arm's length just far enough to bridge the gap but never in grappling stage. Then I am all over them like a rash. I've used this technique all through my life. I figured they weren't martial artists and would rely on the 'cootzee' and whatever brutal strength they had. I immediately got into fighting stance, fists up protecting my face, jaw tucked in and up on the balls of my feet. The biggest one hit Laurie so hard with one punch that he fell unconscious, laid out on to the side walk. Then he turned on me. Once you get used to it. Combat fighting is like anything else. There's no fear. I was never a nervous fighter but more of a full-on brawler not afraid of taking a hit. You develop peripheral vision. No matter what is happening, you turn off the pain, you learn to keep it inside, and you concentrate so you can see what is happening on either side of you. Adrenaline takes over and you get ready to inflict pain. As he came towards me, I hit him with biggest round house kick to the thigh. He buckled over and I see his face light up with pain. I lounged forward with a combination of left jab, right jab and overhead elbows. Circled my arms behind his neck, used him as leverage and started ripping into him with 'Muay-Thai' knees. Nutting him on the bridge of his nose with my forehead. He was grunting heavily as he started losing his balance from the knees to his face. I could smell his bad breath. I kept leaping like a mad kangaroo hanging onto him thinking, don't let go for fuck sake! He started using this same technique on me. Pulling each other back and forth with smashing blows. I felt him jerk back and begin to stagger. But he doesn't fall. He reaches for my long hair which was in a ponytail to steady him. As he caught his balance he started yanking the hair off my scalp. I could feel punches in the back of my head from his mate. Where the hell is everyone else? I thought. I could hear voices in the background, "Noel keep going! Keep going! He's done! He's done!"

I look to my right and see Dean Woodhams fighting for his life. We call him Barney Rubble because he was a short, stocky blonde guy. But he is tough. He is at least a head shorter than the bloke he is fighting and is standing three steps high on the front steps throwing punches at the guy. At least he is keeping him off my back. If it wasn't for him I would be fighting all three. Suddenly, I remember the other two guys in our crew. Looks like they *dogged* (abandoned) it.

It's funny how the mind works when you are in a sticky situation. I feel my hair being wrenched out of my scalp, I can feel his breath but I know as I punch him over and over again in the face sooner or later he is going to let go. The thing is his friend keeps pounding me on the back of my head. Out of the corner of my eye I see a familiar face. John Kizon comes from behind and pulls the other guy off me. He starts getting into him. John was a Commonwealth champion fighter, and I hear the hissing of a boxer. This is usually a sign whether the person you are fighting has martial arts or fighting capabilities. I let them hear every grunt of energy as this works two ways. It rattles the other person and it gives you energy and strength. I know this is the serious side of the business when you finish him off so that there is no retaliation. I set him up for a couple of tile breaking punches. Finally, he is out cold and his hands twist free. I feel the relief in the back of my head and hair. I look up at the sign that says 'Gobbles'. Once again it is the creepiest time of night. The stench of bitumen and the eerie smell of stale piss. The flashing strobe of lights that still sets me off to this day. The yellow part of the night. I think to myself I hate this job. I have been in this spot so many times before. At the end of the day we all learned a lesson. I told Laurie if you want to lead the way, you better have a strategy going into battle. Not long after, he joined the WA Police force. I think he was probably better suited to that job. The other doorman that dogged it were not in Zen Do Kai but Rod gave them the ultimate fanging in the pool house. At times it was difficult to get guys from the club to work on the door. I was grateful my mate John Kizon stepped in and I got rid of the ponytail too.

As I wrestled with Genghis that one fateful night. I thought long and hard about my life. There must be an easier way of making a living. Maybe a restaurant, no security on the door, close at a certain time, endless cups of coffee, quieter environment and nice people. As the months passed, I pondered more and more about moving from Perth. The nightclubs were not my scene anymore. I started to outgrow the lifestyle. Who knows they were probably getting sick of me too.

My wife is from Hawaii and it would make travel back a lot easier. So we decided to relocate to the East Coast of Australia. We bought a small BYO cafe in Brisbane. It had an apprentice cook, three wait staff and a contemporary menu. What did we know about running a restaurant? Nothing. I thought how hard could this be? I was soon to find out. Sometimes you get the feeling you have made a wrong move and you become consumed with thinking about how to get out. Like most new restaurant owners I at first saw only boundless possibilities, all the money that could come in. The food was cheap. The rent wasn't that high. There was an established group of customers. Within a month I found out that this wasn't going to happen. The chef we bought the restaurant left us with the most expensive recipe I ever bought! I put an ad in the paper started looking for a new chef. We were saved. But then within a short time I discovered problems. I may not have known much about running a food business. But I could read people well. So I watched the chef and learned the basics. I figured this business was unlike the security business. The menu was complicated and we couldn't just hire anyone. For someone inexperienced in the restaurant business it turned out to be another nightmare. On the positive end we learned very valuable skills from the chef. I later began to think of it like having one of the boys to teach me all the elements of running a restaurant. Similar to martial arts you learn the basics, observe, have awareness and take it all in. He introduced a Tapa's style menu which eventually we incorporated in our next business venture.

The next concept we developed was something we could have total control of. This time I thought why should I be at the mercy of someone who's going to hold me hostage. I will be the cook. I thought of the kitchen as my dojo. My training ground. While touring in Tokyo I observed the cooking methods in the side street tents. Chicken wire grill and railway track barbeques. So we moved to Cairns up in the Far North of Queensland and started a small cafe and based it on the 'Plate Lunch', the Hawaiian working man's lunch that I became accustomed to while living in Hawaii. I had learned enough to know that I had to learn to walk before I could run. Similar to being a white belt I began the journey again. The idea was to run a street vendor style cafe that did a combination of Hawaiian, Pacific-Asian and Mexican surf inspired food. So we took a little bit of everything and came up with food that was healthier, fun with a fresh vibe. When you are trying to attract a certain market you have to look at all the elements. But because we were in Australia we could take all the elements from Hawaiian tiki bars and funky old surf cafes in Hawaii and push them to the limit because no one was doing them. Tina created the menus based on pupu's or Hawaiian bar food. We tried to do everything with a twist. We made vegetarian fried rice and Asian slaw with sesame soy vinaigrette instead of the traditional 'two scoops rice and macaroni salad.' As Tina developed the recipes and I worked the grill. I found my martial arts background helped me. I was able to focus for long periods of time on what I was doing.

Just as in martial arts you use both sides of the body. I found that cooking was similar to martial arts; it takes focus, concentration and discipline. I also felt this was something that I could do. We were on a small side street in Cairns and little by little I learned to get the feeling for how to cook the food. I even started to enjoy the feeling that after a while I could shut out the world when I was at the grill. It was good for me because I had to shut out. When we refined the concept we re-located to Byron Bay, Australia. Moving here was always our idea. We wanted to acclimate ourselves with the concept first because we always knew Byron Bay would be our final destination mainly because of the similar lifestyle to Hawaii. But I knew the rents were outrageous in the heart of town. After one week of scouting about, someone was closing his cafe after four months. Previously, it was a hamburger joint called Big Blue Cafe, well known for their chicken satay burgers. We couldn't believe our luck. The rent was nearly one half of what we paid eight years ago, we fixed it up with found objects and materials as if you were stuck on Gilligan's island. We called it 'Hulala Café' a Hawaiian Style Licensed Cafe. We would aim our cafe at the surf crowd, make everyone think they were in Hawaii and be the only ones in town chasing that niche. The locals didn't care that the decor came from used tables we found on the street, a few Hawaiian record covers and pictures we had bought from garage sales. They liked it that way. What they wanted is what we wanted. Good food, good vibe and reasonably priced. As I expected running the kitchen was like another kind of street fighting. Whatever happens you have to win. From the time the orders start coming in the grill is hot and the cook has to get everything right the first time.

Each day in a restaurant is different. You never know who is going to come in and whether you are going to have

40 diners or 2. The only way you survive is for everyone to know that all the food you turn out is top quality. You have to be absolutely ruthless to achieve that. No matter what it takes. Whatever people get. It better be good. It took me years to learn how to do that. I would have never been able to do any of it if it wasn't for my training in martial arts.

# CHAPTER 2

# Red Hill Boys are on the Booze again

## Wild Colonial Boys

I was the son of a working class man who shot crocodiles out of a PT boat, raced motorcycles, boxed, drove a semi-trailer and was a full-time mechanic. Naturally, I would follow in his footsteps. As a modern day Bolter we would ride around on British motorcycles and buck the system. All the Red Hill Boys that I knew were drawn to that lifestyle. But there is a price to pay with run-ins with the law. We had to be slightly one step ahead.

Dad was an easy going person who never spoke much and never put any pressure on us. To him the dojo was natural because he had been a boxer as a young man. He was born in Mt. Crosby which is 30 k's from Brisbane and known for the big Somerset dam. His father was head of the Water Supply Department. In his early 20's, he hunted wild boar, kangaroos and foxes in North Queensland. I think he was happiest in the bush with a gun in his hand.

My mum's parents were Irish immigrants who had a big sheep farm in Red Bank Plains, just outside of Brisbane. My grandmother was 99 when she passed away and when she died the property went to the State because my grandfather did not leave a will. Mum doesn't say too much about growing up except she hated sheep and thought they were dumb. There were ten children who grew up in that old house, all boys except for Mum and her sister. Mum was the straight one never smoke or drank; her sister was the total opposite. She drank like the boys and actually died sitting up with a pint in her hand. If it wasn't for karate maybe I would have ended up like that. I think it was a pretty hard life being stuck on the farm with a bunch of rambunctious brothers who wanted nothing more out of life than to work hard during the day and go to the pub at night to get pissed. One of my uncles had flaming red hair and could only go to sleep with his hat on. They were a colourful lot. The sheep and grass are gone. But the memories and the homestead of my family still linger. The Johnston family name is on one of the local street signs and an old black and white photo of my 8 uncles' hang on the wall in a local pub. They were good customers.

Red Hill is in the middle of Brisbane, just 3 k's west of the Central Business District. It's a place of steep hills like San Francisco. It has become a trendy neighbourhood with expensive done up Queenslanders. It wasn't in my day. When I was growing up in the 1950's and 60's it was a place where the working class lived. It was best known for Lang Park in Paddington where the West Leagues Rugby Club played. In my neighbourhood was St. Brigid's church, ice skating rink, fish and chip shops and pubs. It got hot during the summer as it does in Queensland and I still remember the strong smell of rotting mangoes, the meandering river and smelly tanning factories. On my street, cars would be airborne where; all day and night you could hear the zing of English motor bikes roaring up hills. I grew up on the base of the hill called Cochrane Terrace and sold newspapers in front of the Paddo and Caxton St. Pub from an old billy cart. There was an old theatre with hessian seats, a police boys club, swimming pool, an ice works factory, Chinese restaurant and a Four X brewery which was surrounded by the smell of hops so strong I think you could get a buzz by just walking in the neighbourhood.

I was the youngest boy in a family of six siblings. I was always in fights and as a result got assigned to the F class for 'experimental kids'. The older teachers would send the student teachers to see how long they lasted before we drove them nuts. I think that was the experiment. Sometimes the teachers would get so sick of us they would send us to the pool. I think they hoped we would drown. Somehow I learned to read and do basic mathematics. Most of the time I didn't do any homework. It was done for me. Without realizing it, I had worked out my first security business. I was always looking after the usual suspects; skinny, small Asian or Italian kids with something a little awkward about them. Another gang of outcasts who were picked on for having a big nose or eating a different type of food or for just being smart. There were three brothers in my school, who bullied everyone. The older brother was well built and feared by practically everyone I knew. They jumped me one day and the younger brother thought his older brother would easily do me in. However, I kept punching him and luckily he came off second best. After this they wouldn't bother me but would chase this Italian kid, who lived on Petrie terrace near my house and had the same route going home. Of course, he couldn't fight but shit could he run. I distinctly remember the bag of books and school supplies that would bounce up, down and all around as he bolted his way to the giant fig trees. He knew once he made it here he was safe. The house he lived in had two concrete lions proudly displayed on each side of the entrance, fully concreted with no yard. I was invited over one day and remember smelling parmesan cheese for the first time in my life. As a typical Aussie kid, I thought it smelled foul; like stinky smelly socks.

I would meet up with them near the crates of warm milk to collect my homework and give them a bit of a pep talk. Even though I didn't mind trading my bodyguard skills for homework, I made it clear that one day, they would have to fend for themselves. They were so attentive, eyes wide open standing toe to toe with oversized school shorts. More importantly, I stressed to them that they better tone down my homework, or the teachers would soon find out it wasn't my work. At least I was smart enough to figure that out.

My family were accustomed to hard lives. I think that's why I was never worried about getting hurt in fights. Wild colonial boys were the outlaws that ran around Australia like Ned Kelly when the place was run by the British. And even though they lived long before the time I was born I always thought I was one of them, living at the edge of the law. Red Hill was a tough place to grow up and I had plenty of fights. I may not have been much good at school, but when it came to fighting I knew I had at least one advantage- As soon as I got in a fight, a switch went on in my brain that took me into the red zone and all I wanted to do was exactly what I'd practiced under the mango tree. My problem wasn't turning it on. It was turning it off before I hurt somebody. I didn't know then that this was a dangerous quality to have for me as well as for other people.

When I left school as an experimental kid, as expected I joined most of my mates of a select group of kids kicked out of school as a young member of the local gang- The Red Hill Boys. All the University professors do all kinds of studies about what makes kids join gangs. I can save them the trouble you want to start gangs put kids in experimental classes. I guarantee that the moment you turn young men into outcasts they are going to join a gang just so they have someone to relate to. Every year the school system graduates a new class of outcast who have nobody but each other. Then they wonder where the gangs come from. It wasn't a gang by today's standards but we thought we were tough and we got into fights with members of other gangs. If you happened to find yourself in the wrong suburb at the edge of Red Hill and didn't know anybody you had to be prepared to fight or run for your life.

My Dad had won a number of boxing titles and thought that all his children should be trained. I entered my first karate tournament when I was five years old and was disqualified for punching, not using control. This discouraged me but my Dad kept me training and my brother Peter had me run on the gravel without shoes. The loose rocks tore up my feet and he made me keep running. It wasn't your typical kindergarten education. Later on my brothers had me break boards. I think what they wanted was for me to get used to pain. By the time I was 12 years old I had learned certain rules of conduct. Punch first and ask questions later. I knew that if I showed any weakness I would get picked on in the street. I had a punching bag under the mango tree at home and would punch at it for hours, not much for technique but to build stamina because I knew that if I could last three minutes I would win and that was ample time for a street fight. I practiced breaking boards after watching my brothers and sister in the dojo.

In those days a group of boys would hang around the school yard and challenge me to a fight. I could never back down. Later when I thought about this it appeared to me that I learned martial arts for all the wrong reasons. Martial arts is about self-control, about avoiding fights and about being confident no matter what people say. If you really know martial arts fighting is always the last resort. But back then I didn't know any of this. I wanted to be able to walk the streets of Red Hill with my head high and get respect from other people. One look and it was on fuelled by meat pies and adrenalin. The thing I learned was if you get into a fight you have to have a plan. The bullies would come in talking and pushing and making noise and expect you to roll over. The more I got into fights, the more it became reflex. I had a pretty easy life hanging out with my mates, going to school and getting into scraps. This phase of my life ended when I was about 14. Gary, who was the smartest one of the 'usual suspects' bunch, was getting cornered by the head bully in the playground. He was getting nailed but I waited before jumping in, just so he could have a taste of what it feels like to cop a bit of a hiding. When I finally pulled the head bully off, I told him he was weak for fighting someone who he not only outweighed, but couldn't fight. "I'll have a go!" I said. He copped several good jabs until his eye closed up and he had the biggest black eye ever until he cried, "I give in!" Having a go was my speciality along with my mango tree technique. I wasn't about to let Gary down, but I did tell him that one day he would have to learn how to stand his ground.

The school headmaster called me in sat me down and said "Noel you don't have to come here anymore!" So I didn't. That was my graduation. At least they kicked out the other kid too who tried to beat up Gary. My parents weren't outwardly upset. I know my Mum wasn't happy. Perhaps I would have been expelled if I didn't have anyone to do my homework for me. As for the fighting no one really expected anything different. It was part of the neighbourhood. There were only a few rules. If you get picked on, fight back. And whoever hits you, hit back twice as hard so they don't come after you again. The other rule was never let your mates down. Following is a list of the core group that made up most of the Red Hill Boy's gang. Additionally, there was also many 'hanger-ons' that came around like flies.

## Boo-Boo

I hung around with "Boo-Boo" who had the same features of a small round bear. He had curly wire-like hair which he continuously tucked behind his ears. I think he wondered why he even had ears. Everything he did was with pure gusto and no social skills whatsoever. He was the annoying one, who would open your fridge and start drinking all your beer. No one ever wanted him at the party as he would plonk down in the middle of the lounge and include himself on your conversation. He was the mad one out of all of us, who started 99% of all the fights. He rode his motorcycle like a dirt bike up and down stairs doing wheelies through the steep hills off Bramble Terrace. His real name is John Ruksentas who worked as a boiler maker at the Brisbane wharf.

## Mangos

Kenny Bryant was one of the biggest kids in the school... Everyone was scared of him because of his size, but he was never a bully. In fact, he was the comedian of the bunch. He is blond, brawny and built like a rugby player. He used to pull the concrete rollers around the tennis courts to flatten the grass and just for fun to build his trapezoids. He got his name 'Mangos' because his trap muscles replicated large mangos. When I started touring with Jimmy Barnes, I ran into him in the lift of the Hyatt on the Gold Coast. Today, I hear he has a worm farm in Tewantin, QLD.

## Specs

"Specs" wore a black long trench coat and dark rim thick glasses. This look was unassuming because he was the most vicious fighter of all. He was dangerously quiet.

## Chicken Wings

Trevor Harrison hung with Specs and wore the black trench coat with military-style boots. He was solid but couldn't hit the side of a barn. He got his name from the wild flurry of swinging 'Chicken Wing' punches he'd throw in a fight.

## The Ryan Brothers

Vernon, Dennis and Koeki Ryan were half-Greek and half-Malaysian who were all phenomenal boxers. Their father was a champion boxer who used to sell fancy shirts at the pub. Their mother was a great cook of authentic Malaysian food. Vernon had a panel-beating business next to the Red Hill Hamburger shop.

## Zoobie Ken

Kenny Allman, skinny, blond, quiet kid was staunch till the end. His parents were so happy that we accepted him into the group. He drove us everywhere in his metallic blue EH panel van. I'm not sure why I called him 'Zoobie'. Probably because you had to warm him up to get him going.

## Mud Guts

'Mud Guts' was a big overweight kid who snacked on live bugs. He'd carry pray mantises' in his pocket and pop them into his mouth to stir people away from the keg.

## The Two Martins

Martin Rowntree, tall model-like looks, tattooed and could fight well considering he looked like a pretty boy. Martin Craven was a skinny nice guy who could mix it in with best.

## Red

'Red' a big bulky guy with long red hair, had a very bad stutter and we almost always finished his sentences. He couldn't fight very well but always had a coat full of weapons. He hung mostly with Specs and Chicken Wings who looked a sight in their long black trench coats.

I became initiated into the Red Hill Boys by accident. I was waiting outside my brother Peter's judo class, at the dojo near Lang Park. A guy I knew from school, Daryl Watson used to tell everyone we were brothers. He approached me and I thought he was being friendly. Then, I sensed that he was turning on me. Following him were about a dozen of the Red Hill Boys. It must have been Daryl's initiation if he beat me up, he would be accepted in their gang. I dropped my paddle pop that I was just finishing up when he started to shape-up. The mango tree training worked. He landed in the cactus and I went hell for leather. I was fearful the rest of them would jump me too and I had hoped my brother's class would finish so he could help me. Instead, they ended up slapping Daryl and started to giggle as they wandered off down the road. I was always weary and avoided them as much as I could. However, I was running into them on a regular basis. I can still recall trying to time my visits to the fish and chip shop. Not long after that they were calling me over to drink beer, watch the footy, and crash parties. However, I never bought a long black trench coat.

## Never tell the Red Hill boys there's a Party

We used to sneak into the school dances and if we didn't get in we would drink beer in the panel vans outside. So like a lot of young people with time on their hands and no particular thoughts about the future. We started tinkering with British motorcycles recklessly riding around Red Hill like rambunctious hooligans looking for trouble and entertainment. Which in our minds was pretty much the same thing. We were always looking for a party to crash, whether it was in Red Hill or in the neighbouring suburbs. One thing you should never do is tell the Red Hill Boys there's a party and you're invited. The craving for action became a kind of addiction and often felt that once we got to the party everyone would like us anyway. They obviously did not have the same aspirations that we did. The party is in Ashgrove not far from Red Hill. We meet at the Paddington pub. We tried to enter through the front door which leads to the back courtyard. A guy tells me to get lost. I'm taken back I thought we were all likable. They were all a lot older, but probably underestimated us. I proceed towards him and pull his shirt over his head (a trick I learned in the street). Mango tackles him to the ground and says, "I wouldn't let him in either." We plough our way into the backyard, the music is blaring and there is a mango tree next to the keg where everyone hangs. I see a dozen or so heavily tattooed guys. This is where it always goes down. I check where all the jugs and glasses are as this is usually the first thing they grab and then it gets ugly. I'm approached by a big solid guy. He doesn't waste any time talking. He lunges at me with a barbeque fork and grazes me. I retaliate with a head butt and groin kick I can't believe I drop him. I can hear sirens and know that someone has called the police. Everything erupted. I glance over and everyone has taken their positions back to back. The other guys are attacking us. Chicken Wings is throwing a flurry of punches connecting with us as well. The Ryan Brothers are fighting with their boxing skills. Mudguts is ploughing into them using his body weight. Boo-Boo is floating at the edges, picking off the retreating ones. Zoobie

Ken is hitting them with anything he can lay his hands on. This is longer than I anticipated. I hear Mangos grunting and growling throwing full-on head and body shots. The two Martins have arrived and start to frenzy on every guy in the place. Even though we still hear the police sirens we know they won't come till it's over (they figure let them kill each other first). I look over and see Spec's glasses broken; I'm thinking someone will pay for that. We start to spill out onto the street. Of course this is where we feel more at ease. One guy starts mouthing off the balcony and we yell out "Red Hill Boys are on the Booze again" I look down at my boots and there is squashed mangoes (I think my world revolves around mangoes). All of a sudden there is an eerie silence we all jump into the panel vans and head back to a Red Hill house. We turn the music full bore. Later we hear the guys at the party were "Black Panthers". We were obviously on their turf.

## Red Hill boys in Surfer's Paradise

I didn't know anybody who went to University. People did trades if they were lucky. Most were working class people: tilers, dockers, mechanics or drivers and if they couldn't do trades they worked for the Council painting or digging ditches. After work, men went to the pubs. We all came from working class families. Most of us had nothing. They say the more you know the less you need. Of course, we all thought we knew everything. "Pack the panel vans were heading to the coast!" Boo-Boo wants to go surfing and here's our chance to get away from the city. One carton of beer per person should be just enough to lower the suspension of the car. I giggle as we beg, borrow and steal surfboards and think how funny the poser's of Red Hill have turned into surfies with tattoos, jet-black hair, and kicking boots. It's all a ploy to have an opportunity to drink at the Surfer's Paradise beer garden. Dennis nearly drives over the cliff in Greenmount and Zoobie Ken has already drunk his quota. We hit the waves one by one, waxing our boards looking like a bunch of hoons at the beach, except for Mangos he's the only one with blond hair. I see Muddy stranded on the rocks and Chicken Wings is drifting out to sea. Mangos is fighting with someone who dropped in on him. By the time they hit the shore they both have blood pissing out of them. I say you should stick to street fighting you probably won't get hurt. Just one more thing to do; we chase a few surfers up the beach that had been in a fit of laughter coming back to the van. "I'm never coming back to the beach again." says Chicken Wings "Give me Red Hill and the smell of rocket fuel any day." We are in full form by the time we hit the Beer Garden. Rod Stewart's "Maggie May" is playing in the background and Boo-Boo is arm wrestling some body builder. I whisper some coaching in his ear. "You'll never win, arm wrestle with your left hand and when he puts the pressure on, hit 'em with your strong right punch." I'm surprised he listened, as he hit him so hard he starts running towards the wall of us. He is followed by his muscle bound mates. We crowd around ready to get it on. Spec's yells out "Body builders are all pooftah's!" Like a scene from a bad western movie he picks up one of the bar stools and cracks it over the heads of one of them. I wish they were playing better music. Zoobie Ken belts out a verse again, "Red Hill boys are on the Booze again!" We get it on with the lot of them and once again we are back on the streets. We part with Boo-Boo's famous saying, "Never mind, I know where there is a better pub. We'll be liked there." Boo-Boo and I would head down to Byron Bay or Tweed Heads when we had the urge for rice pudding, beers and on the odd occasion a fight in the pub.

## First Job at the Drug House

My auburn hair started getting longer and longer. Besides beer, I wanted to buy a western shirt and a pair of jeans. At the age of 15, I got my first break. I had been getting into fights and mum wanted me to stay out of trouble. She saw an ad, for a job at the Drugs House of Australia. It was a pharmacy distributor that packed boxes to be sent out to all the chemist in Queensland. She told me to get a reference from one of my former teachers. I asked Mr Owen's and to my surprise he supplied me with one. Before I left that day and took it down to Montague Rd. in West End, my mother gave me a stern warning to stay out of fighting so I could make something of my life. I had no schooling card, no credentials of any sort and no real knowledge of the adult working world other than what I saw in the movies. So after I fill out the employment form the big boss sits me down and puts a children's puzzle in front of me to see if I am at least smart enough to put the different shaped blocks in the right places. 'If this is all it takes to get a job I should have left school a lot earlier.' What was I thinking? Then came a moment of fear. I had seen a similar puzzle used in the movie 'One flew over the Cuckoo's nest.' It suddenly occurs to me he might be thinking the reason I don't have a school card is because he thinks I'm stupid. Does he think I am an idiot? To my relief, I put all the pieces in the right places and the boss thinks I'm all right, I'm hired. I am the official dispatch clerk. There is a conveyor belt, I put things in boxes, I weigh them and put them on the belt and I'm getting quite good at the job. I follow everyone to the canteen for morning tea, lunch and afternoon tea. I love my lamingtons and vanilla slices. I really wasn't sure what I was supposed to be doing but I figure if I just pay attention I will pick it up- so I follow everyone else. I show up for work every day on time and after a few weeks I get really good at what I am doing and try to be as efficient as possible. At times I actually jump on the conveyor belt and run back with products to speed up the process. Everything is going great. And then one day I see a guy who much older than me, picking on a young girl named Betty at the canteen on her first day of work, she breaks into tears. I watch him make her cry. So the next day I wait for him at the front wall and tell him to lay off. He told me to "Piss off; I'm not scared of you." The red light goes on. I only know a couple of things in my life at this point. Don't pick on girls and make sure you are the first cab off the rank. So it's a couple of jabs and unfortunately I broke his nose. (unfortunate for him) I return back to the conveyor belt as if nothing had happened.

I get called in to the office by the big boss but he does not have a puzzle for me. He asks, "What happened?" I tell him that guy was picking on Betty. I am thinking I'm in trouble. Remembering what Mum told me on the first day is going on in my head "Be punctual, and for god's sake don't punch anyone!" I think this is it. I'm probably done. I'm fired. However, he does not let me go. In fact, maybe he likes me. I think everyone in the canteen is happy he finally got what he deserved. Nobody could stand him. However, it is still a bit tense in the canteen so I go across the street for my lamingtons and vanilla slice. I stay on the job and although I am reminded everyday as I pass the brick wall and see a blood stain, the boss still smiles as I pass by. I work alongside an older guy who is in charge of the area where I am. After about a year, I get called into the bosses' office. Only this time he says "Noel, we want to give you a promotion; to be in charge of the area you are working in now. But I knew I was taking someone's job. I shook my head and said "No thanks, I don't want it." The thing that always kept all the misfits together was loyalty. We may have been different and flawed individually, but we always stood up for our mates. Then I left the boss's office and got back to work. I sensed the older guy knew what was going on. I could sense his fear. I told him straight up I didn't want to take his job.

I must have enjoyed this job because I recall putting money every week in the kitty to save up for the yearly Christmas party. But then I make my first serious mistake, I invite Boo-Boo along. Before that I managed to keep my work life and the Red Hill boy's separate. The party is at a Function Hall and as usual he's pissed, boisterous and gets into a fight with someone outside of the party. Everyone hears about it the next day. He complained about working as a Boiler maker and begged me to get him a job there. So I stupidly make my second mistake and get him a job there too. I managed to hold onto the job for eight more months. But Boo-Boo turns out to be a bad influence. We would go to the pub for lunch and just as we were ready to go "C'mon lets have another one. We can always run back." But we sometimes staggered back late. It soon became clear that drinking and conveyor belts don't mix. Boo-Boo was always opening the effervescent tablets and chewing them up with water. Lunches were getting longer and longer until eventually we never went back. Thanks to Boo-Boo my career was ruined. Who knows I could have been there happily for the next 30 years or possibly until I became redundant.

## When Salt and Pepper Met

Most of our time was spent going to the rugby league games at Lang Park. The Red Hill boys had a special dusty dirt patch on the hill. We never paid to get in; we would jump over the fence. The security would let us get away with it most of the time. This special area became the no-go zone for practically everyone else. This was our territory; we could buy beer and Bundaberg rum and holler like a tribe of wild animals having a hell of a time. We sometimes got kicked out for fighting with other gangs from other suburbs. It didn't matter we would sit on the roofs of houses nearby where some of the boys lived. Chanting loudly, 'The Red Hill Boys are on the Booze again!'. Mostly everyone avoided us. Until one day a tall blond surfer kid named Rod and his friend Nicky were shouting out at us. "Fucken wankers!" We thought these two 'dick heads' were mad, stupid or drunk. Just the two of them looking for a fight without a care in the world. We pelted our empty beer bottles at them but they still carried on. In the spirit of Red Hill, we ran down the hill like Custer's last stand and mowed them to the ground. They got a real hiding from us. A picture was posted in the Courier-Mail of Rod Stroud and Nicky O'Callaghan titled 'Red Hill Boys are at it again'

Soon after, Mangos and Rod get into another fight at the Newmarket School Dance. Not many of the boys were around and Mangos bit Rod on the arm before the fight gets broken up. We all wondered, who does this maniac, blond surfie kid stomping around on our territory picking fights with everyone thinks he is? The boys are on the hunt.

The regulations and laws were pretty laid back so most of us were let into 'The Wave', a city Nightclub next to an old digger's pub. Mangos and I go to the loo to take a leak and we spot Rod. We start to size each other up and give each other a smirk. My first instinct was to let him have it. I wait for Mangos to give me the nod. However, he thought Rod and I had similar mannerisms, just two crazy kids looking for a bit of respect. Before we get into it Kenny says, "Let's just leave it at that, and let bygones be bygones." We head back to the bar and after a few drinks we realize Rod is just like the rest of us.

Arthur Symes, who hung out with us on occasion, lived alone in a block of commissioned flats. It was a typical old and run down fibro-type boarding house, comfortable to fit all members of the gang, shoulder to shoulder (if we had a party). If there was a swimming carnival going on next door we would all be yelling out like it was the local footy game. We named the lady living next door, the 'Ouija board lady.' She was constantly calling me over to read my fortune. Probably could see great things for me; lots of potential. I invited Rod, Nicky and Wayne to a Red Hill boy's party one early Saturday. I was keen to introduce them to the rest of the gang and smooth out any bad blood. Rod walks past the Ouija board lady. She calls out for him. But I yell back, "You can't save him!" Rod fits right in as he places his back up against a wall. The music is blasting and the energy is fierce. Nicky and Wayne look a bit more awkward. Nicky doesn't wear his glasses and can't see without them, but doesn't want to look like a nerd. He locks eyes with Spec's and thinks maybe he should have worn them. I wave him over and he bumps into Mangos and bounces off him. "You right? You need glasses!" says Mangos, Nicky weaves his way behind Wayne trying to look for a place to stand. He accidentally steps on Karen's foot. (Mangos sister) You could tell they wanted to discreetly leave but knew Rod would kill them. This was the first meeting after Rod and Kenny got into that fight. Everyone was still a bit gun shy. There is a loud knock at the door. Nicky sees me open the door to a jolly-green giant of a guy and his followers trying to crash the party. I am thinking there is no room for you and if I let you in, you will be eaten alive, bones and all. "It's a Private Party" Does he listen? obviously not. He still insists on trying to come in. Mangos is the first one to the door to rugby tackle him and the rest of us start sinking the boot. There is race for his mates. The boys are in a flurry to pound them. Nobody can hear them groaning with the music blaring, swimming carnival screams and Ouija board lady yelling out "Bad Karma!" Boo-Boo, still with a drink in his hand chases after the jolly-green giant as he ran into the Newsagency screaming, Help! Help! We hear the familiar siren and jump and hide in the bushes till Boo-Boo gives the all clear. We get back to the party and wonder why anyone in their right mind would want to gate crash a

Red Hill Boy's party in the middle of the day? Perhaps they should have seen the Ouija board lady first.


"Neighbours drooling, looking out
for the fool at the front door

While clowns inside are sleeping in their beds

Knowing there's no safety behind four walls

Meanwhile Red Hill Boys outside
are bouncing off the Walls

As there's a rumour it's their last call

Make sure you don't head for the front door

They'll come at you full bore

So whatever you do don't open the war

because there's only one law

Red Red Red Hill Boys are on the booze again"

CHAPTER 3

# The Way of the Red Dragon

## Heading for Four Walls

Because we weren't allowed into the school dances, we started to go to the pubs and drink with the older working class men. Once I got turfed out of a pub by the doormen. There were only two of us against 10 laying the boot into us. Mango's sister (Karen) jumps in and starts to trade blows with the doormen. I've never forgotten what she did for me. I was so battered and bruised that I nearly lost my eyesight. It was one of the biggest hidings I ever received and I knew that to give one out, you'll have to be able to take one too. We were 17 at the time so we had a lot more lessons to learn. Lesson #1 was keep your mouths shut and learn to fight better.

I don't know when I first started to feel the hum in my head. That is- thinking about what I'm doing now and what I'm doing next and what can go wrong. When you're raised like a Rottweiler on a short leash you're trained to attack when the red light goes on. You don't worry what's going to happen next. Your adrenalin takes over. The biggest worry is that you're doing everything you were trained to, up until that instant. I never worried about getting hurt. Most of the boys I knew of didn't live to 25. I didn't expect to either. When I was growing up our slogan was "Die young and leave a nice corpse."

My life was working, going to pubs, getting thrown out and then going back the following week. As times were changing, so were we and the reckless fights over nothing had become more and more dangerous. We were starting to realize that these big brawls in pubs were no longer just your average street fight. Sometimes I'd look over at the big fat guys sitting with their beers at the pubs, not a penny to their name and nose's red from alcohol and a different kind of red light went on. I thought if I don't change that's going to be me. I started getting tired of the whole thing and wanted more for my life. I didn't know how to do it. We were physically working on the council, training, and along with this came the fact that you could actually hurt someone. My mum said she had enough and didn't want me hanging around the Red Hill Boys. Luckily, I was working on the council laying pipes, digging ditches and building man-holes with Mangos and Zoobie Ken. I started working alongside Grot and Snot, two brothers who tried to recruit me into their motorcycle club, 'The Norsemen.' Although, we became good friends, I opted out of that lifestyle after spending one night at their clubhouse. Mum and Dad took a liking to Grot and Snot, who were often invited for Sunday Roast. I often wonder where I would be today if I followed that lifestyle.

# Zen Do Kai- Way of the Warrior

Rod had started training in Zen Do Kai Martial Arts and wanted to recruit some of the Red Hill Boys. He knew we were all good fighters. Slowly, I saw less of the Red Hill Boys and started to hang around with Rod. We would soon find out most of them declined, not wanting to comply with a karate school and be disciplined. They were more interested to stay on the hill and drink rum. Rod asked me to come down to check out a grading at the Honbu located on Elizabeth St. in the Brisbane CBD. Until this point I had only heard about Bob Jones concept to Martial Arts. A Street-oriented Self-defence school, which takes the best of all the methods and blends it into a Freestyle Martial Arts. I had seen pictures of Bob, but never met him. He had long red hair, drove a 1970 bright red 2-door Ford Coupe, airbrushed dragons on each side with illuminating eyes and the words 'ZEN DO KAI.' It was impressive, it was a beast. Bob Jones worked as security for Fleetwood Mac, The Beatles, The Rolling Stones, Stevie Nicks, Joe Cocker, David Bowie and had most of the security contracts for nightclubs in Melbourne.

After the grading, Rod and I piled into Wayne's car for a drink at the pub. At the light near Roma St., I notice three guys terrorizing a homeless man in the park. I immediately jump out of the car and charge after them. I attempt to knock them out with a couple of flying round house kicks. They all scurried away in enough time before the police arrive. As we stood there trying to defend a helpless man, the police suspect that it was Rod and I who beat him up. Luckily, I was saved by a family picnicking in the park who told them what really happened. I also did not realize that

Bob Jones was following in the car behind us and asked me how I learned how to kick. "I learned off my brother Peter who was a Judo instructor." This incident pulled me more and more away from fighting in the street and training in the dojo. Prior to Zen Do Kai I didn't have any real structure to my life and found the dojos provided it.

I started to learn the true method and meaning of Martial Arts. You start at white belt and learn all the basics and when you reach black belt this is considered the beginning. Bob Jones gave me a black GI when I was a white belt as a sign of strength. I won 8 tournaments in a row and was also awarded the Bushido Cross as a demonstration of loyalty, dedication and strength. At last I felt I was doing something with focus and discipline. It instilled an incentive for me to maximize my efforts to gain acceptance in the 'new family of security.' The cross also exemplifies commitment to the protection and instruction of the brothers and sisters in the ranks of Zen Do Kai. When I reached 2nd Dan this grading was absolutely brutal. It is considered the Warriors dan. It starts with a warm up and 5 Katas. Bob says just turning up on the day is a sign of immense strength. He knew that everyone was going to be extra tough on 'Crazy Noel'. He wished he charged a door fee and if I had known better I would have trained harder. You line up to fight 30 x 2 minute rounds-- all fresh black belts with no rest in between, until you reach the 25th round when I fought Bob Jones. It was 40 degrees and the dojo was packed to the rafters. The vegemite sandwich I had that morning was now stuck in my throat. During the earlier rounds my shin guards were so soaked with sweat, I decided to remove them and cop the kicks on the bone.

As the grading progressed I could hear a chant from the audience. "Crazy! Crazy! Crazy! Crazy! This chanting and seeing my Dad shadow sparring in the stands fuelled the fire to keep me going. I fought Rod in the 1st and 30th round. During this time 2nd Dans were brutal beatings. Currently, they may be similar to a triathlon.

## Unsavoury Mince

My family moved to Woolloongabba, which is 3 kilometres from the CBD. Every day as I left for work on the council, the neighbour's dog would bite at me. This went on for months. Mum would usually make some dinner for me after work and before I left for training. Today it is Savoury mince, an iconic Australian dish and a lamington, an iconic Australian dessert. I sat down and started to complain to Mum about the dog. She was hesitant to leave me alone but made me promise to let it go. I was a volatile 19 year old, which meant letting anything go was difficult and having a go was easy. "Yeah, Yeah" I promised. It wasn't the dog I was so annoyed about, it was the neighbour who would stand at the top of his stairs and laugh. As usual he sat half way down his stairs drinking a can of beer smirking at me as I looked out the door. He was a real yobbo in his tight blue stubbies and matching singlet. As soon as Mum left, I took one more bite of my savoury mince and made my way down the front stairs. "Get over here you wanker! I outta beat the shit out of you, and that mongrel of a dog!!" He walked towards the edge of the fence and must have had a bit of Dutch courage. "Oh yeah? You can't fucken touch me, I'm on my property!" as he takes another swig at his beer and gives me a solid smirk. My eyes dart around to see if anyone is watching. "Oh Yeah? I can fix that!" I reach over, pull him over the one meter fence like a keg of beer and wrestle him to the ground. I start to lay into him as the dog is barking and biting me in the back of the neck. I start to head butt the dog too and I hear a neighbour yelling out from across the way. "Leave him alone! Leave him alone!" Another one of the neighbour's dog charges after me from across the street and starts tearing bits off me. In the heat of the moment, I grabbed it around the throat and we clash heads. By now, the neighbour is flat on his back and the dogs have run back to their own havens. I hear another neighbour yelling at me from his door across the street. I start running, but he quickly slams the door in my face. I punched my fist through it few times and feel the adrenalin and blood rushing into my eyes. I walked back and the neighbour must have got himself up and retreated back into his house. I feel a little bit better as I walk back up the stairs and finish my savoury mince and lamington. Shortly after that Dad arrived home, "Jump on the back of the Norton Dad, let's go get some beers." He seemed surprised as usually I was off to training. I give the Norton a kick start and Dad jumps behind. We both know the guy at the bottle shop. "Hey Noel, how are ya today?" "Good!" I replied. Dad holds the bottles of tallies between us as we head back to the house. I turn on my sister's stereo and put on the Rolling Stones. Dad and I sit down at our 1950's retro vinyl kitchen table just down the hallway of the front door. In this era, everyone kept their doors open, so anyone who came up the stairs could see dad and I having a beer. I start to tell him a little about what just happened. I could tell dad anything, he never pressured me to be this or be that. He always just let me be. As a fridge mechanic people would give him free cartons of beer all the time. He'd come home staggering to mum's nagging but never said much. No matter how hung-over he was he always made us breakfast.

We both notice the police sirens seem to be getting louder and louder. The police come charging down the hallway to the kitchen with their guns drawn. "Get your arse up off that seat!" (Their gun's pointing in my face) Dad yells out, "Hey enough of that! No need to be so aggressive!" Mum, is clearly upset, "It won't be long before you get locked up and they throw away the key!" They've called the Tactical Response Group or TRG and closed off the street. The police arrest me straight away, throw me in the back of the paddy wagon and take me down to the watch house. I was processed, but the neighbour did not press charges, probably felt sorry for my mum. Rod showed up wondering why the streets were closed off with so many police vans. We found out, when one of the neighbour's called the police, he mentioned that he saw my 2$^{nd}$ Dan grading and would need more than just a paddy wagon. After this incident, I never saw my next door neighbour again. I wondered where all the other dogs have gone, the streets seemed very quiet.

## British Bikes and Bits

I bought my Norton Commando from British Bikes and Bits, near the Weetabix factory. I remember the smell of burning sugar cane as we rode our bikes flat chat through the streets of Woolloongabba. The harrowing turns I made around the corners would cause a vibration that snapped the bike stand. So I placed my helmet carefully under my bike as we park in front of the bike shop to use the pay phone. This was not ideal and would eventually cause the foot pegs to snap which were not cheap to replace. It was not the only thing to snap; the bike crashes to the ground and snaps the foot pegs once again. I start to beat the shit out of the bike with my helmet. Rod is desperately trying to block me off from seeing the guys across the road but I spot them bowled over with laughter. I start taking off straight towards them. As if in slow motion, they start to panic and pull the huge chain down attached to the roller door. All you could hear was the chain crackling down and they see me getting closer and closer as they desperately pull at the roller door. Rod is trying to pull me back with no such luck. As I reach them the door slams down. I can hear them in there as I swing my helmet at the door. Rod footy tackles me and drags me off. They must have known I was the "Savoury Mince" guy.

## Extreme Blonds

There was a small group of guys who travelled around the same stomping grounds. Rod had confrontations because his girlfriend Kathy had spoken about them on a few occasions. Now when you just mention something to Rod it can set him off in a good or bad way. Of course, no matter what he always included me. If it sets him off, Noel feels the same way too. The 'Extreme Blonds' were skinny, gothic-looking guys with matching tattoos and peroxided hair similar to Billy Idol if he had a bad hair day. The six of them stood out like dog's balls and walked with a vampire swagger. To the untrained eye you would probably pass them off as transvestites. However, we knew they meant business with their assortment of utensils bulging under their jackets. This is about the time when street fighting had taken a U-turn, and was not a rite of passage to get you out of the burbs. It was quite simply put that you don't have to train or put any effort into it, just carry a weapon of choice. Tonight, a few of us are playing 21 at Wayne's house. Rod, Nicky, Wayne and I plan to go out afterwards. As usual, Rod loses a few games and tips the card table up a few times. Kathy calls Rod at Wayne's house and tells him the queer-looking Blonds are here at the East Leagues Club, and they've been touching her up. Well, they must not be queer, but attracted to blonds. She calls him out to fix it. "Noel, you're coming right?" "Keep your shirt on, she's you're bloody girlfriend." He turns around, clenches his fists as tight as a drum and bares his teeth. With the combination of summer heat, poker and rum, you can't even cut the air with a knife. I push him to the side as we step into the front yard and pile into his sandman panel van. We called them pie wagons because of the small fan on the roof to let out the hot air and steam. Rod is driving like a maniac, and Nicky and Wayne are rolling around the back like kegs of beer. He slams on the brakes and Nicky flies to the front. "I didn't do it on purpose" he says. Rod is the first to jump out of the car with his chest already puffed out. He adjusts his belt, does a couple of shoulder rolls and says, "Let's get em" Kathy sees Rod at the front entrance, "Any longer and I would've done it myself" she snaps. Kathy tells us they are near the *loos* (toilet) and we follow her in. Although, the club is packed and dark this crew is literally glowing in the dark. Kathy hurls abuse at them and Rod steps in and punches one of them in the eye. The rest get a bit of a touch up but nothing too out there. We were out of there in what seemed like under a minute. As the months passed, and Kathy and Rod would routinely break up and get back together, one thing stayed the same. If ever Rod was out and ran into anyone of them, it was usually on, with a black eye here and a black eye there.

One day, Rod is having a snooze on the lounge after work; before going to train. There is a knock at the door and he gets up half asleep still in his bricklaying stubby shorts. He opens the door and a fist comes flying through to Rod's nose. He rides it out and starts to retaliate with his usual punches and kicks. He realizes as he comes to his senses, it is the six-pack of blonds. They start laying straight into Rod, upturning some of the furniture as Rod's parents are watching T.V. Rod's mum, slowly turns her head and says, "Now enough of that Rodney!" The blonds start to back up a bit. She makes the blonds pick up the lamp and furniture and demands Rod to say sorry to them. Of course, Rod doesn't answer and follows her to the kitchen. "I'll make a cup of tea and you boys work this out in a peaceful manner" "What? Don't make them a cup of tea, they're not staying!" She brings out Rod's favourite 'Iced Vovos'(shortbread biscuit with pink frosting laced with coconut flake) and starts handing them out to the blonds. Rod is mumbling under his breath, teeth still clenched, "don't give them my biscuits!" I arrive shortly after and am amazed to see Rod and his new set of friends. "I thought you were the only child?" Rod glares at me and says. "Your fucken funny aren't you." One guy tells Rod, he was sick of getting black eyes. So after numerous attempts from his mum, Rod finally gave in and says, "Aw right, so I copped a punch on the nose, fair enough, you had the guts to come to my house to sort it out let's just leave it at that." I asked Rod, "have you ever thought of owning a hair salon? I reckon you'd make a fortune." Rod growls at all of us, and throws his fist in the air. His mum catches him and barks "Rodney now you behave!" After a few years we find out that one of the extreme blonds married Mango's sister.

## Painters and Dockers

The "Moon Bar" was next to the Honbu, separated by a dark brick alley. The owner and a majority of the doormen were in Zen Do Kai. Of course, Rod and I felt at ease amongst these surroundings. We were not really into the disco scene, but we drank there anyway. There was a steakhouse on the bottom and patrons would go upstairs for dancing. We always started drinking early on Fridays at the Brook Hotel, a workers pub in Mitchelton. We forgot that when you reach town you're supposed to be mellow to fit it with the disco scene. On entry, big Noel Hatwell, greets us in. "No dancing to Kung Fu Fighting" he says, it scares the suits. It was a sight to see the boys out on the dance floor doing kicks and katas to this song. The patrons would scatter desperately to the wall. We make our way up through the bar and join a few others for a Friday night drink. After all, we earned it of course, training hard; working hard it was all part of the Australian Psyche. We notice a group of guys sizing us both up. Wrong place, wrong time, young men their eyes crazed with alcohol looking for a punch up. There is an old street fighter's saying; the fight you pick is normally the one you lose. I can tell Rod is thinking the same thing. Usually, he stirs his rum and coke with his finger. They wonder why we have not answered there taunts. We try to avoid them by heading towards another part of the club to finish our drinks. As we head downstairs to try and leave, we remember Nicky is with us too. "Don't worry about him, Rod says, "He's too pissed anyway." They follow us to Rod's HK Holden panel van. The half dozen of them start to circle around us. Rod and I are back to back like two peas in a pod. We are already in the zone. They are tooled up with bottles and a tyre lever. "What's your problem?" Rod says. "Go fuck yourself!" says the guy with the tyre lever. He takes a swing and Rod side steps with a huge lunge and bangs him straight on. He drops like a sack of potatoes. We manage to fight off the next two with a barrage of punches and groin kicks. We give the next three some warning punches and let them take their friends away. As they reach the end of the alley, they start to mouth off. "Our fathers are Painters and Dockers!! We'll fucken hunt you down and get you back!"

Rod and I brought attention to the club with our drinking and brawling at all the nightclubs. At one stage we were nearly banned from everywhere. Although we weren't angels, I know we didn't start many of the fights. However, we thought we'd try this wine bar on Queen's St. where all the suits went. We fit right in drinking Mateus and eating all the free bread sticks. Eventually, we even wore our welcome out there. Our reputation for carrying on was either "Good for the Club" or "Bad for the Club". However, Bob always knew that if you needed guys to come to the party. It would be Rod and I. He called us the "Rottweilers of the style".

A few days past and we hear through the grapevine that the Painters and Dockers have put a hit out on us. "How much do you think they would pay for you Rod?" I thought dead or alive maybe a couple of bucks. Why would they even bother? Rod and I could really care less. Bob wanted us to split up and move states. Rod decides to go to Perth and open up schools. There was no way in the world he would go without me. But we tell everyone else I'm going to Adelaide.

## The Treeless Plain

The Nullarbor Plain was a little more than a dirt track in the early 1970's. The aboriginals named it the Treeless Plain, because it went for miles and miles without any trees. In some places it was raw, rough and dangerous because of the road trains full of livestock. Sometimes with three or four trailers you smelled them before you could see them in your rear view mirror. It was a rank, dirty and dusty smell of cow manure that you could smell for miles away. When you heard the roar coming, you just move to the shoulder and let them pass. You don't fight with the road train. Especially on dark nights when there is no moon. Wayne Ogden was a soft spoken, brickie working with Rod. He trained with us at the dojo and he too wanted a change of scenery. Rod and I on the other hand, were full of adrenalin, adventure and wild bolters. Luckily, Wayne was the sensible one to balance us out. I tried to convince Rod not to bring his gun. He was adamant and pig-headed and wanted to be a cross between Daniel Boone and James Bond. Initially, he wanted to get back at Kathy's (now his ex-girlfriend) new military boyfriend. I don't know who to believe when Rod tells me, he was threatened. Luckily, I talked him out of that one. Otherwise, then we'd really need a good reason to get out of Brisbane.

Wayne agreed to drive to Perth under strict instructions. One, he would not let Rod and I drive and two, he would not drive any faster than 60 miles per hour. He was proud of his surfie-looking lime green Holden sedan. Luckily, he planned the whole trip. We would make our way out of Brisbane through Northern New South Wales. Head west through Goondiwindi and make our way to Broken Hill. Travel through Adelaide and straight through the Nullarbor to Perth stretch. Rod and I were happy with whatever Wayne had planned, we were just looking forward to drinking and having fun. He wasn't kidding about not going over 60 mph. "Even if you go one click over the speedo, you could possibly not even make it" he kept repeating.

I was squeezed between Rod and Wayne in the front seat. All the gear in the back, cartons of beer, a bottle of Bundy Rum and bags of clothes and training gear. As Wayne cautiously drove, we swigged our beers, while Rod shot at metal signs and anything that took his fancy. Dodging the clatter of Rod's brass .22 calibre shells bouncing off the windscreen, I would sneak my foot on the accelerator to try to get the car to go over 61 mph. "You could possibly blow the cylinder heads" Wayne repeated. We dodged wallabies, wombats, cows and a few kangaroos as they would stop and get hypnotized by the headlights. Many of these animals will sleep or lay on the road, which absorbed heat in the winter. They were probably heading for the side of the road near the gullies where there is water. We stop again for another piss on the side of the road. Rod takes a puck shot at one of the kangaroos. It drops to the side and Rod thinks it is dead. He stands near it and takes a leak. Suddenly, the kangaroo leaps up and catches Rod off guard. "Rod you're a fricken idiot, it's a harmless animal, how'd you feel if you got shot" He quickly back-peddles with his zipper half-way down. I jump the kangaroo and start sparring with it. This is the first time I've ever boxed with a kangaroo and hopefully the last. It finally hops back on all fours, spins it's rather large thick tail and retreats back to the bush. As I watch it hop away between the ghostly gumtrees it turned back and gives us the 'evil kangaroo eye.' I hope he doesn't come back with his mates to even the score.

Our next stop is the petrol station in Moree. It is a town which just borders Queensland and New South Wales. I still can't believe we have not even made it out of Queensland. It seems as though we have been driving forever especially with the 60 mph compliance and Rod going fully ballistic with the gun. The shells are not only flying everywhere, they're smoking hot. I am literally clowns to the left, jokers to the right, stuck in the middle. After Wayne gets out of the car, I slide out on his side and decide to be responsible for pumping petrol. I pull the bowser off and petrol spills over my shoes. I'm thinking, this is just bloody great. Sparks from hot live rounds combined with petrol isn't a real smart mix. What if we burst into flames and no one would ever find us! Rod slides out of the seat, brushing the empty shells out of his top pocket of his prized plaid flannel sheep-lined jacket. I give him my 'evil Rottweiler eye' and he glares back at me with his 'evil wolf eye.' So I jump on his back and give him a few punches to the head. Out of the blue I notice a metallic Ford LTD doing well over 100 miles an hour. I yell out "slow down idiot!" Rod tries tackling me back, "I Love you like a rock Noel!" We jump back in the car and I break out into my favourite Rolling Stone drinking anthem, "Time.... is on my side... Yes it is...Time...is on my side." We drive pass a small mob of kangaroos hopping and scattering up across the road. We all spot the metallic LTD again, this time on a bit of an angle in a small gully. I belt out, "Beware of Kangaroos!"

Wayne is feeling a bit tired and decides to find a spot on the side of the road where we could sleep for the night. We drive until we see a semi-trailer parked to the side. It looks like a safe resting spot. Wayne intensely studies the map while Rod and I fight over who gets the back seat. "Too late, I'm already sitting here!" I said. "No dramas, I'll find a nice spot on the side of the road and sleep like Daniel Boone!" He stumbles out of the car before catching himself off balance. Drunk and incoherent he sways in a circle and slurs, "Hand me my gun." I reach beside and grab it by the barrel and the stock. I see his silhouette from the flashlight that Wayne is using and carefully pass the gun. "BOOM!" I clench my teeth and feel my brain bounce from side to side. The piercing sound rings my eardrum. I try to swallow the ringing. It is pitch black and I try to picture the sound fading. Then I hear a familiar voice. "Am I Shot?!" Rod slurs again this time a bit slower. Wayne whips out of the front seat and throws me the torch as if it were a hot potato. Even though I am just as drunk as Rod, I cringe at the fact of seeing blood or guts. Luckily, Wayne packed a torch even if it wasn't real flash. No stupid boy scouts on this trip. Rod stood there patiently, didn't look like he was in any pain and I couldn't see any blood. So I slowly inspect the area around the upper thigh half way up from his groin area. Rod and Wayne look down and wait patiently in the dead of the night. I notice a very small spec of a hole through his jeans. I put my index finger around the area in question. Again, I cringe at the thought of what his leg might look like on the other side. I shine the light a second time and stop half way up from his groin. "Ah, oh...um... yeah, I think it must've got you." I looked again just to confirm the confusion bewildering in the air. Feeling a bit like a doctor now, "Um... ah... yeah your shot, I can see a small hole" He starts to take his pants down, opens his arm like Jesus on the cross and collapses back into the red dirt and yells out, " THE INDIANS ARE ATTACKING!... Quick light a fire! Light a fire!" As he fell to the ground we could see a cloud of red dirt dust. The semi-trailer parked near us starts up quickly and drives away. I scratch my head and start to get my senses somewhat together. "Wayne, let's put him in the backseat." Then Rod's speech becomes even more impaired, "I remember seeing this in an old western movie, I'll bite down on a piece of leather while you burn the tip of the knife and use it to dig the bullet out." Sounds like a great method except, we don't have a fire lit, nor do we have any necessary supplies and two-thirds of us are blind drunk. "Let's go to the nearest hospital" says Wayne. Now that sounds like a better idea! He jumps straight in the car to get a better look at the map. The torch is just not cutting it so we drive a bit further up to get some light. We believe we are in the middle of nowhere but, if we can figure out where, we could probably find the nearest hospital. We stop at a streetlight crossing to get our bearings. Wayne and I try to figure out where we have to go. The map is a total blur for me but I feel I must try to focus and desperately try to sober up. Luckily Wayne is fairly calm and taking control of the situation. Rod sits up and looks out the back window at something he hears. "Hey, where are we?! I think we better get off the tracks! That's a bloody train coming our way! Wayne gets us quickly into gear and off the train track! Clearly, he is now a bit shaken, "Whoa! What the fuck that was so close!" The live rounds have temporarily blown out all of our ear drums. We catch our breath in disbelief and organize our thoughts again. Wayne knows we have passed Moree and prefers to drive to the next town instead of back tracking. I definitely think driving back to Moree would put us back even further on our trip. So we come up with another great idea and head to the town of Narrabri. It is probably another 40 minutes, but Wayne caves in and says he will go a little over the 60mph. At least we have drinks to numb the pain. I'm not that worried about Rod as he seemed comfortable enough in the backseat. I know he is probably thinking perhaps the gun wasn't such a great idea after all.

We pull into the town of Narrabri and follow the signs to the hospital. It is your typical small country town, one hotel, one hospital and three pubs. Wayne and I make our way to the front desk of the quaint little country hospital to tell the nurse our mate has been shot. Rod slowly makes his way limping up the stairs as his leg starts stiffening up. By now he can hardly walk but we watch him struggle towards the big country nurse. She grabs a wheelchair, plops Rod down and folds his knee in half. "OW Shit!!" he screams out. He grabs his thigh and glares at us. We try to hide our mouths as Wayne and I start giggling. Then she asks, "Who the hell shot him?" My eyes widened and lips close but I didn't answer. Rod is damn lucky I just missed the crowned jewels. But of course, Rod starts pointing the finger at me, like I did it on purpose. Yeah, I may have shot him but it was his fault too. After all, it was his gun and who's the idiot shooting at anything and everything. She really has no time for our drunken antics. "Go to the police station and see the Sargent!"

It never dawned on me that the police might think I wanted to shoot him. When Wayne and I got to the station the Country Sargent asks, "Who shot him?" I was bit coir, but admitted "I did." "Were you trying to kill him?" "No, it was an accident." I said. "Were you shooting at anything?" he said. "No, not really", (hoping he doesn't check the car full of empty shells) "Where's the gun?" he says. "It's in the car." "Go and get it" he orders Wayne. The police must think we are all lunatics. Especially when Wayne brings it back and literally points it towards them. "Hey! Hey! Don't go pointing that gun half hazardless!" He asks about a gun license. "Um, license? Ahh...we don't have a license." He opens his top drawer and starts filling out a form. Then he charges us $5 dollars and takes the gun off of us. No worries, I wasn't about to get into any arguments. Wayne and I leave the station and go back to see Rod in the hospital. "He won't be getting out tonight" says the nurse.

So the following morning Rod is in full form. The pounding hangover is worse than the actual bullet in his leg but clearly not as bad as being stuck in the children's ward with some noisy patient. Not enough beds for adults. His arms folded up like he was forced to eat sour grapes. Wayne and I could not contain ourselves with laughter seeing Rod in the oversized children's cot with his bung leg hanging over the end. Things were not going well, he was not only complaining about the old bloke next to him moaning and groaning, but his favourite plaid sheep-lined jacket went missing. "Fucken hell, this ole' bloke is driving me insane." "I'll just have to fly over to Perth from Brisbane and get me Parent's to pick me up." His face all scrunched up and eyes howling like a wolf. We calculated the whole trip would've taken us through three more states and about 4462 kilometres. We barely made it across the border from Queensland to New South Wales or approximately 525 kilometres or 5 hours before Rod getting shot. "I hope this old bloke doesn't keep me up all night!" "Oh well, looks like it'll be just Wayne and I." I quietly chuckled.

Rod calls Bob Jones to tell him about the minor setback. However, to his surprise, he has already heard what had happened. Bob says, "It came over the radio, you were shot by the Painters and Dockers." Rod laughs, "It wasn't them, it was bloody Noel!" Word was spreading around the club like wildfire about Rod getting shot. Everybody was certain it was the Painters and Dockers. Rumours had been spreading for many, many years following this story repeated at summer camps, backyard barbeques and whenever one or more first generation Zen Do Kai members were in a room. To this day, it is still a mystery about the hit man for the Painter and Dockers, found dead in his LTD, which was mobbed by kangaroos. If you were lucky enough to hear this story told by Rod and I, after one drink too many, you would have felt the epic thriller of a blockbuster movie.

As Rod hobbles his way out of the hospital on crutches, he suggests to his Mum and Dad that they stop at the local pub for a counter lunch and a pot of beer. The usual fare consists of Bangers and Mash or if you're lucky on a Sunday, a Lamb Roast with three veg. Just when things aren't going well his eyes light with pure joy when he spots a guy sitting at the bar with his favourite plaid flannel jacket. Not a very big town. Without a blink of an eye, he hobbles over, leans his crutches against the bar, grabs his jacket and pulls it down off of him. "Give me back my jacket" says Rod. The guy doesn't put up a fight even if Rod is on crutches. (Probably could tell by the madness in is eye) Rod slides his jacket with pride between the hole of his crutches and turns to see his mum behind him. "No counter lunches today Mum, we'll have to stop at the next town."

If you are game enough and have the urge to bolt across the Nullarbor Plain, in the land of UFO's, brumbies and kangaroos; let's hope you don't break down in Wilcannia knowing you only have beer and bad manners on board. It's long empty road, past mining towns, road houses and aboriginal communities. One by one, as we past these remote towns, we wonder about the abandoned American military base in the middle of nowhere. At least it's a quieter trip without Rod. When Wayne and I emerged from the outback and came to the part of Australia where the ground stops being red and grey and starts being green. I thought to myself this is alright. I saw the big buildings of Perth in the distance and came to a stop. It was my first real look at Australia and a world bigger than the one I'd known.

# Chapter 4

## Salt and Pepper

Wayne and I found a two bedroom flat across from Scarborough Beach Hotel. I thought it was a lovely spot with white sand beaches right at my doorstep. It was a 1970's brick veneer with a million dollar view to the ocean. It seemed a world away from the city pavement in Brisbane. Rod arrives soon after with the hollow point bullet still lodged in his upper thigh. He is quite proud of the bullet and compares it to the old wounds of a soldier at war. Sometimes I piggy back him from the dojo when his leg stiffens up. No wonder the cops called us 'Salt and Pepper.' We start to establish the Zen Do Kai Perth dojos and they are quickly starting to boom. Our students in Perth were a broad spectrum of people from all walks of life. Surf life savers, women, kids, lawyers, bikers and even to my amazement the police. Our reputation soon gets us work in many hotels and pubs-- and many of the Zen do Kai boys came over from Brisbane to live, train and work. Rod and Wayne were both *brickies* (bricklayers) so we got a lot of building work around the place. Perth was going through a construction boom and it was easy to find work. When we weren't working we were running classes and building up Bob Jones Corporation.

## Soccer Hooligans at the Thornlie Hotel

Georgie Russell was a hard-core, notorious bouncer from Brisbane who got us work at the outer suburb pubs. They were the venues that no one else wanted. They were basically biker bars where they came to get drunk and into violent fights for a night of entertainment. They say its sex, drugs and rock and roll-- in our world its alcohol, fights and rock and roll. It was hell for the owners. The places were full of broken glass and very lazy safety and licensing laws. Once again, police always waited till it was over before coming around. We were asked to put some order back into the venues. So there it was total irony- at the time I did not even know the meaning of the word. We left Brisbane and our tainted reputations to help clean up the pubs in Perth. It was some of the worst venues I've ever been to. As reckless as we were we handled the situations that came to us. As usual, we went hell for leather. There was no turning back. This is when the code of the Bushido came into play. The brotherhood of Zen Do Kai gained more and more strength.

The Thornlie Hotel was one of our first gigs. If your car was ever stolen just drive out to the car park and you'll be sure to find it there. It is still true to this day. In fact, years later around the early 90's, Tina parked the "Tuna Boat" (Holden Station Wagon) near the train station in Perth. The car was stolen and a few days later, someone reported it abandoned at this very same pub. I drove this car while working the doors just in case some punter ever got the shits with me. We hated the Thornlie; it was the roughest English pub in Perth. Rod and I were one of the only few who were stupid enough to run the door here. It was full of soccer hooligans, skin heads and punk rockers. As soccer hooligans they all had there set corner-- English, Irish and Scottish. It was just the two of us in our corner, back to back trying to sort it out. As the session progressed so too the banners would fly, chants would echo and closing time erupted into full on brawls. I hated the ten minutes to closing time countdown. They would bulk buy the drinks and sit there abusing us for having to kick them out. This one soccer hooligan bought half a dozen beers and sat there antagonizing me with the countdown, mouthing off. "ten minutes...nine minutes...eight minutes...what the hell are you going to do about it?" I admit I wasn't a very patient person, so I looked at Rod knowing this guy is going to cop the biggest hiding. By the time he hit six (my lucky number) I hit him with an overhand tile breaking right punch. He did a mickey flip back. By the time the police came, the place had emptied and we had gone home. We were always outnumbered in this pub and they knew it.

## Maylands Dojo

I opened the dojo in Maylands and it attracted a Motley crew of students. However, when we were all in the dojo it was a humbling effect. It shows that no matter what your background or lifestyle choice the dojo brings one common ground for anyone who wanted to empower themselves by learning self-defence martial arts. We got to know a lot of the bikers through the pubs we were working at, this worked hand in hand with us trying to promote the style. It was how we all connected in those days. The Coffin Cheaters had there club headquarters in Bayswater not far from Maylands. Some of our students such as Frosty, Irish, Marbuck and Peter Creen were the first to come over from the Odin's Warriors in Brisbane. The bikers had a similar code to Zen Do Kai and therefore were attracted to the workings of the style. If you are running a biker bar it was only natural to hire bikers to run the door. They walk the same walk and talk the same talk. I was approached by Eddie Whitnell, from the Coffin Cheaters about doing private lessons to about 50 of his club members. I thought this was unusual at first, but agreed since he was a good mate. "I'll do it as long as they don't call me Bruce" I said. We formed respectful partnerships through clubs, nightclubs and outdoor concerts. Obviously, it was not a traditional martial arts class. They all had an art for street fighting but wanted to improve on their technique. They had members who were already black belts in Zen Do Kai and had total respect for myself and the art.

## Cold Chisel and Current Affairs

Australia wide Bob Jones Corporation had started to go for international acts, festivals and rock concerts. During this time Midnight Oil, INXS, Cold Chisel, Party Boys and the Divinyls were carving their careers in all the pub barns. These days live music was everywhere. This was total chaos the fights of throwing punches, chairs and people who want to hit you with broken bottles. After a while we got rid of all the crap venues and started running the bigger nightclubs while building the martial arts academy. We did a Cold Chisel show in one of the old theatres in Perth; the promoter had failed to advertise and only 300 punters showed up. Jimmy Barnes thought great, 'let's throw a party!' He closed the doors and paid for the open bar. His brother John Swan wore a bushido cross and he was a good friend of Bob Jones. After the show he invited all the security to the hotel for more drinks and all night partying. After this we would always pick Jimmy and Cold Chisel up from the airport and take him to all the nightclubs for free drinks. Cold Chisel didn't have much money while touring, all tightly held by management and promoters. Rod had a natural ability to run business so between the two of us we ran a tight security business. Many of the other styles and security companies didn't want us around. We were getting most of the all the contracts in town and dousing the competition. Perth was now our territory. Bob had stayed in touch with us and would fly over to attend grading's and visit the dojos. We had yearly summer camps which were a week long gruelling training session of seminars, grading's and special classes. We also had special self-defence classes for nurses, cab drivers and television stations.

Terry Willisie, who was doing Current Affairs, started training with Rod and I. We did a segment on re-enacting violent crimes and how with a little bit of self-defence knowledge you could get yourself out of a sticky situation. Everyone thought we were just a bunch of lug head bouncers; this cemented the good we were trying to spread in the community. The nurses were very appreciative of the self-defence lessons and many of our women students have actually been in altercations and were thankful that they had some self-defence knowledge.

## Potato Chip Bandit

Rod and I were preparing for the annual five day, Zen Do Kai summer camp held in Albany, WA. Bob Jones, Malcolm Andersen and a few black belts from around the country flew in. In order to handle the intense and gruelling summer camp, you not only need to be physically prepared but mentally as well. Basically, you eat, sleep and breathe martial arts. We were doing combat training, sparring, running with a tire strapped to our waist and teaching classes. So once again, we decide to have a night out to celebrate all our efforts. Rod has a brilliant idea to ask Peter Sadler's wife, a hairdresser to give us both Mohawks. He talked me into it even if I knew you didn't need a hairdresser for this particular style. What are best mate's for? Rod was adamant and I didn't want to ruin the party. She finished in ten minutes and we stand side by side looking like a couple of chick magnets. We all head down to the Scarborough Beach Hotel. Frosty and Marbuck are working the door and nearly everyone whose anyone, knows about us and how basic things work. That is to say nearly everyone except for one group. It still amazes me how common sense usually is left at the door. If you see twenty rough looking guys standing around a bowl of chips, you would have to be unconscious of the consequences if you reached in and grabbed some. Chances are you're going to get bits ripped off you. However, this guy who is a heavy-set brick layer reaches in and grabs a handful of chips. I thought he just made a mistake. Some of the boys are much more elaborate and think this guy is committing suicide. Rod looks at me and says, "If he takes one more chip, he is dead meat". In slow motion he grabs one more potato chip and just before he puts it in his mouth, Rod snaps it out of the air smashes it to crumbs and says, "Buy your own chips!" I'm thinking these chips must taste pretty good to get killed over. "Fuck off!" he says as he half shapes up. His mates catch wind of what's going on and start to cluster around him ready to mix it on. Again I wondered, if I saw a collage of bikers, large fuzzy haired Maoris and two guys sporting Mohawks with crazed looks in their eyes, surely you would make a wide berth. But he attempts to throw the first punch before Rod plants him with a few good ones. This erupts to a full-on brawl. There were a few advantages of knowing the doorman. It was easier to get them out with a few take away punches for the road.

When you get into as many brawls as we did, you don't think about them until you get the 'copper knock' on the door. Brash and obnoxious, Rod and I have heard this knock many times before. A few weeks after summer camp our Mohawks look ridiculous and off they come. We get a loud knock at the door. Surprise, surprise it's the local CIB asking Rod and I about an altercation that occurred on Friday night a couple of weeks ago. Always prepared and ready to go, Rod has his questions and responses down to a pat. Similar to shampooing your hair, wash, rinse, repeat. "Are you charging me? Have you got a warrant? No comment. Are you arresting me? No comment. Have you got papers?" This infuriated them as they begin to fill in the blanks about an assault at the Scarborough Hotel, where Rod's name is brought up. We figured it was the potato chip bandit. The police couldn't figure out who had the Mohawk. "Wasn't me" I replied. The potato chips were not only tasty but costly as well. In court, the potato chip bandit cried over not doing anything and that he was innocent for getting assaulted. Rod pleaded his case and told the magistrate how he felt totally intimidated by these big, brawly-looking brickies. The judge probably thought, he should have bought his own chips and ruled in Rod's favour. It is the case of "One potato chip too many." Barnesy and I were at a bar and he showed me his special way of eating potato chips. Open the top and splash worcestershire sauce about 6 times. Close the bag and shake it up. "It's a meal." Jimmy says.

## Once were Soldiers

Tony Renata, like many of us, grew up fighting his way through life. Born in Auckland, New Zealand he later became a champion kick boxer in Australia. He trained with Rod and I in Brisbane after crossing over from another style. I drove him across to Perth in my red mini cooper S, and remember waking up in the middle of the Nullarbor thinking I was still driving. Although Tony never said much, we seemed to always be fighting about something whenever he was around. This usually meant, working side by side at the Maylands Hotel seemed suicidal. Rod and Tony are having a few drinks at the Herdsman Hotel and INXS were playing a live gig that night. Although I still smell of sweat and tiger balm I join them straight from the dojo. After a few hours into our session, Tony gets into an argument with a guy who is mouthing off about Zen Do Kai not being a recognized style. We were often confronted by other schools mainly because of our freestyle approach to martial arts. Bruce Lee was known as a free-style martial artist and of course, today Mixed Martial Arts is everywhere. They start to surround Tony and he bangs three of them in a multiple attack. Rod and I start tuning up the ones coming towards us. We figure if they want action, we are the door to knock on. Rumours began spreading about how we jumped the guys from a Kung Fu school and Tony punched up one on crutches who was partially disabled. They wanted revenge and the head instructor calls Rod to set up a meeting with the intention of sorting it out. In those days, most of our students were Maoris, bouncers from the east and bikers. Like the movie, Once were Warriors, it was one in, all in. We meet at the Surf Life Savings Club in Scarborough and Rod coordinates our strategy. Irish on the roof top, ready and waiting if they are armed. Peter, Marbuck and Frosty who are used to getting it on, especially within a large group are with us up the front. I was hoping that Tony, Monty and a few of the other Maoris with 12 inch afros would be enough to scare them off. But Irish spots them coming over the embankment ready to mix it on. I notice the solid-built Asian leader, front and centre with about 30 of his guys. He wastes no time at all, "Your guys beat up one of my students and put shit on my style. Who is running this style?" he says. "I am" Rod replies, and steps up. But he points to me and says, "I want to talk to you." We edge towards each other and in a dead silence moment, someone drops a baseball bat off the wall. We immediately get a bit jumpy. One of them yells out, "I'm going to get my shot gun!" We point to Irish on the roof, "Don't bother because by the time you get back it will be all over." I look him straight in the eye as we stood about a foot apart and said, "This is what happened, that guy was mouthing off to Tony about Zen Do Kai and in the heat of the battle he bangs one of your guys in crutches. As you know in war, things happen but we never put shit on your style." I see his shoulders drop and he turns around and gives his guy a disappointed look. That was it, all for nothing. When we parted we made sure he knew in a roundabout way that we respected him for standing up for his style and defending his honour. He made his way up to the embankment and gave his student a big hiding. Steven Siu (who was the head instructor) and I became good friends as the years past. We would always meet up at the Sebel Hotel in Sydney while on tour with Jimmy. The last time I saw him, I invited him and John Cullen, the other famous Bush Lawyer, to my hotel room for a drink. I think Steven knew that one drink would lead to an all-nighter and 10 hours of Crazy Noel stories. So he quietly walked behind me made sure I got to my room and ran off down the hall. I later hear the controversial story of John Cullen, found dead with a needle in his arm.

## Kampuchea Benefit Concert

"Concerts for the people of Kampuchea" was a series of concerts held to raise money for the victims of war-torn Cambodia. The event was also filmed (subtitled Rock of Kampuchea) over 4 nights held in Hammersmith Odeon, London. Paul McCartney and Kurt Waldheim (who was then the secretary-general of the U.N.) organized well established artist such as The Who, Elvis Costello, Wings as well as new wave acts such as The Clash and The Pretenders.

The promoters held a smaller concert in Fremantle, Perth. Around the same time we were recruiting and training a new generation of black belts. Some of the original members were retreating back to their home state, apprehensive about commitment to this lifestyle. This was definitely not the wonder years as such. It was peppered with scars, stitches, barmaids, booze and brawls which was usually followed by compulsory black belt classes after a graveyard shift. No doubt this would continue by recruiting more black belt potentials through mid-day sessions at Scarborough Beach Hotel. It was our "Local" and recruiting black belts was a full-time job. In between the drinking sessions and fighting to 'Wayne Green and the Phantoms' we often tested black belt techniques in the pub. In the dojo we did not tolerate weakness especially if you make it through the bottleneck of Nidan (2nd Dan). I still remember when we trained for this day. We built up our stamina by running in steel cap boots holding a house brick in each hand across the Story Bridge in Brisbane hoping to pass the pain barrier. We did push ups with our knuckles until they bled in order to build the mind and body. We hung posters to promote the style everywhere; in convenience shops, laundromats, fruit and veg shops and health food stores. There were pictures of Rod and I with the katana in hand. The dojo house was literally a stone's throw from the police station and they knew exactly where to find us.

At the concert, we all wore our bright yellow BJC martial arts t-shirts so we would stand out in the crowd. It gave the illusion there were more of us. The cleanskins all huddled in as we covered all areas. Perimeter and gates manned at all times, unless the walkie-talkie system comes into play. We have a limited amount of man power to watch the fence jumpers so we rotate the positions every 30 minutes; another technique to show we have more man power. The promoters set up the alcohol marquee in the middle of the football field. Everybody is clued in regarding the red, yellow and green code. Usually, if a situation is ready to erupt we shout out the code and location. We just get word that a group of bikers drove straight through to the front gate and have barraged their way to the marquee filled with people drinking at the bars. I shout out over the walkie-talkie "All hands on deck, all hands on deck, code red, middle marquee!" Rod and I get there and it is a notorious scene; bottles and tables flying everywhere with the noise loud enough to entangle the ropes. I jump clear on one of them, straddle a table and dive at him on his bike. He falls just outside the marquee. When I catch up to him, he gets up, I ankle sweep and judo throw him to the ground to get him in a serious choke hold. The other bikers, jump off their bikes in a panic fashion and start to shape up. I yell to everyone, "Close off the circle! Close off the circle!" Rod covers my back or open side, as I have one knee on his solar plexus with just enough room to keep him conscious. It's a "Billy the Kid" technique we've seen as kids in the movie. They are scruffy bikers, which looked as if they've jumped out of the rubbish bin; torn, worn out and smelling like road kill. I yell out, "Anybody steps forward and I will strangle the living daylights out of him!" Out of the blue, one of them holds up a baby, "look they hurt the baby, look what they've done" Rod is clearly disturbed, where did the baby come from? So Rod yells out, "The police are on their way!" He starts pointing his finger in the air to let the crowd know. I knew they wouldn't be able to control them but I release the bozo I am holding down anyway. He can hardly walk back and staggers along with the rest of them. They start to retreat to their bikes and their usual bullshit abuse starts flying thick and thin. Rod is livid; seeing blood red. We gather information about them. Jock, one of my black belts' tells us that about twenty of them are squatting in a house nearby. I recall seeing them at the Maylands Hotel and best of all they drink at the Scarborough Beach Hotel Sunday session and hang right by the pool tables. They are not wearing any colours. This puts Rod in an unstoppable state of mind. I see his mind ticking overtime. He is on a mission to road kill. All week he is peaking, benching an enormous amount of weights followed by aggressive shoulder rolls and breathing through his teeth. As we run up the hill from hell, I mention again about all the posters of us again. Karate experts, bodyguard to the stars, combat fighting and best mates with Crazy Noel. No worries, easy access to find as well. He wonders why I am so casual about everything acting like it's just another day in the office vibe. So I suggest we go to our favourite health food shop up the road where we have been funding for years. Healthy wraps, carrot and ginger juice everything to balance our hard-drinking and fighting I suppose. Rod loves this place, he says the same thing to me on every visit, how it is such a simple concept and he is probably making a million dollars. As usual, he parked his bike right on the side walk like he owned the place. Like clockwork, he orders his little treasure of healthy fare and sits down facing the glass window to see who is looking in. By this time, I had already moved out of the dojo house. Similar to a nightclub, I am sick of the comings and goings, sick of the numerous big hangi holes in the backyard, of living a stones' throw from the police station and getting harassed nearly every time I ran down the road. "Do you really think it is a good idea to be so adamant and go after these guys?" I asked again. Rod being in true form finishes his carrot and apple juice like a magical elixir and says, "You're with me right?"

We both worked at the overflow on Saturday night incident free. Just the usual drunken slurs which consisted of "Why can't I come in you fucken wanker" "Come on, one on one, I'll beat the shit out of you" "I promise I'll be good, please let me in" The next day, the phone rings, "Noel, its Rod mate, you ready?" Rod was notorious for including me in everything anyway. Generally, he'd say, Noel doesn't like you either. "Yeah, I'm ready" It is the Sunday session so I put on my black overalls for a meeting with some undesirables and slip out the back door down to Rod's place. Of course, he is waiting impatiently donning his black overalls as well. It is a Salt and Pepper moment. We walk down to the end of the driveway and I see only Ronnie (aka Kamai) in the driver's seat of the car. He is chain smoking with a nervous twitch. Ronnie is a quiet Queensland country boy, who came with us on one of our road trips. "Are you up to this?" I said. "Yeah, but Rod said to just stay in the car and if you need me I'll bring the baseball bats' in" I turn to Rod and say, "Where the fuck is everyone else?" "Fuck 'em, don't need 'em" Rod jumps in the front passenger seat and I in the back with the assortment of baseball bats. I visualize the scene unfolding, three guys, two mad ones, one getaway driver going into battle with a pub full of bikies. Somehow it is not looking bright. But we had nothing to look forward to either. Ronnie still looked a bit sheepish as he pulled in right in front of the pub driveway. I could tell he didn't want to come in just by the way he tapped the steering wheel. Rod jumps out and does the customary rolling back of his shoulders and warms up like he is at the gym. He takes off and is clearly ahead of me but I know where he is headed. I take three deep breaths and snake my way through the crowd to the similar smell of B.O., deep fried chips and stale beer. My shoes even stick to the carpet. It is packed to the rafters and I lock eyes with a couple of hippie chicks with that stereotypical musk smell. I see Frosty and Marbuck and hope Rod gives them the heads up. But instead, he goes straight to the pool tables. This is not the place to be reckless every fist is adorned with rings that convert into knuckle busters. I'm fully immersed in it now, walking through bikie territory of leather jackets, thick belt buckles and pointy boots. No hesitations, no room for second thoughts, no second prize, if you snooze you lose. For Rod it's just road kill, he spots the culprit that held up the baby. "You tried to do us in, turn the crowd on us! Why did you hold the baby up?" Oh so now I know why he is so uptight about it. Angry at what *could* have happened, not what did happen. He is the only mad person I know that thinks this way, besides me of course. Why the hell would anyone be angry at what could have happened and is willing to sacrifice his one friend in a sea of smelly bikies. He grabs him by the hair and drags him through to the front door. Surprisingly, his mates step back. Even the crowd is clued in and gives Rod plenty of room. I follow him and tell his mates not to move or else and follow Rod protecting his back at all times. We reach the roadway at the top of the driveway and Rod ropes the dope with him. I yell out, "halve the circle, halve the circle, I got your back mate." I am in fighting stance waiting for the on slaughter but nobody steps into the red zone. Frosty and Peter Creen fill the rest of the circle and Ronnie jumps out of the car with his hands up at anyone who moved. Rod finishes the bikie off by bouncing him off the bitumen. Just like that, as quick as a flash, we are back in the car. Kamikaze Rod satisfied with the result, he finds closure.

We have fond memories of the Scarborough Beach Hotel our "Local". In just a few years they trashed the hotel before it finally closed making way for fancy beach front hotels. Today, it is probably lined with luxury condos with ocean view penthouses with modern names like "The Vue" or "Discovery". For us we kept going, Racecourse shows with Cold Chisel, Angels, university gigs with Split Ends, Punk Rock and Skin Head venues with a dash of running the Underground nightclub. Subtle gigs were added to the mix such as Leo Sayer, Richard Marx, Flash Gordon and Sandi and the Sunsets. Work was everywhere and so were we.

## Madness comes to Town

We had the contract to do the security for Madness, who was one of UK's biggest chart bands of the 80's. The promoter, Michael Chugg booked them at one of the better Perth Theatres. At the time, we thought this venue was more for Ballet or a classical show. He wanted more bums on seats and brought in all these extra plush velvet chairs. We tried to warn him that they were destructive pommies-- a nice mixture of punk rockers and skinheads probably tooled up with razor blades. Our motto for this show was

"Keep them Calmer, Strip off their Armour." They were notorious for wearing their Doc Marten's with Red laces. We knew this meant they drew blood with they're kicking boots. We tried to shrink the doorway entry by standing on each side and only letting them through once they took their Doc Marten's off. I figured without their boots, they might be less likely to play up. I was wrong. We piled all their boots in the front foyer and kept them out of sight. We told them we would give tickets for them. They threw bricks and rocks through the front foyer and broke the front glass. We had our work cut out for us. Especially Tony Renata not only was he one of us, he was from New Zealand. Skinheads hated Non-Whites. As the show went on, Tony was standing near me in the front of stage. There wasn't a pit, as this is where the extra chairs went. He was getting spat on and abused I kept telling him to move more towards the back. (in other words don't stand next to me) I could feel the 'madness' in the air; something was about to erupt. The crowd was getting rowdier and rowdier. We were on our toes in the front when we noticed the crowd starting to leap onto Chuggie's precious velvet chairs and onto the stage to rush the band. There was about sixteen of us who hopped onto the stage standing on the balls of our feet in fighting stance and knocking off these crazy skinheads off the stage. It became a full-on brawl and I thought what hope have we got they are even attacking the band. I looked down and the lead singer was under my feet with his black top hat covering his head. The lights came on and the skinheads must have figured it was time to go. Luckily they started retreating back into the foyer and out the door. Then the riot started again when they remembered their boots. One of the bigger skinheads confronted us about his Doc Marten's. He threw a couple of punches and I laid him out. We had all of their boots just above this stairs and started to throw them over the balcony. They were howling in there strong English accents, "Where's the other side to me boots!" Many of the skinheads were threatening to kill us when we left. We tooled ourselves up as we left near an alley way behind the theatre and saw a car pulling slowly along the side of us. We were certain it was retaliation but it was the boys in blue instead asking us if we were off to a baseball game. You could tell by the look in their eye they knew what went on but as usual showed up late and drove off in the other direction. We all celebrated that night in a true bonding session. All 16 of us stuck together and stood up to the mad, crazed and raucous skinheads. The next day on the front page there was a photo of the skinhead, holding up one side of his boots. I should have sent in the quote "Keep 'em calmer, Strip 'em of their armour" The velvet chairs were ripped to confetti. I remember Michael Chugg saying those fucking velvet chairs cost me a fortune.

## Narara Music Festival

Bob Jones Corporation had the contract to do security for the Narara Music Festival. It is a suburb located in the Central Coast of New South Wales about 54 kilometres north-east of Sydney. This was 1982, all the Perth boys flew over to Sydney and Malcolm Anderson from Queensland brought his crew which included 40 Rottweilers. Malcolm was Bob's right hand man who had a breeding kennel of Rottweilers. For the concert we set up a double fence and had the Rottie's surround the perimeter. This was to keep the festival goers from jumping the fence. Someone had spread a rumour that the first 100 people to show up at the entry gate could get their money back. We thought this would start a riot and gathered all the dogs with us. What a sight to see about 1000 punters all scattering back from the vicious barking dogs. At the time it seemed a bit primitive but it worked and it looked good for our image. The concert was held for 5 days and we all bunked in military beds on site with the dogs. As soon as the concert started the heavens opened and it pissed down raining like cats and dogs. We ran it like strategic martial arts operation and confiscated alcohol, sharp objects and anything imaginable, including jars of vegemite. Towards the end of the concert the promoters were doing anything to keep the water in control. Lightning had struck some of the scaffolding and mixing equipment. We were all in a meter deep of water and Talking Heads, one of the headlining acts refused to go on. When it was Cold Chisels time, Jimmy belted out "Were going on!" You can always count on the wild colonial boys of rock and roll. Jimmy didn't care about whether electricity and water don't mix. The camping ground became one big party as people congregated in there special groups. The bikers had a bonfire and kept to themselves. Some of the hippies tripping on acid and heroin were doing there tribal dancing up the front in the mud and water. Next minute they would fall over and get taken away by ambulance wrapped up in aluminium foil like a human hot dog. We all celebrated with the confiscated bottles of alcohol and endless supply of vegemite. We booked a cruise ship after the concert. There were 20 of us running amuck on this ship. We had a tug of war contest with some of the Sydney

CIB. What an irony, stuck on a ship with 20 other cops. They were pulling so hard on the rope, I told everyone 'let go' and they all went flying backward into all the deck furniture. After this concert, we were getting offers to run more and more festivals and the security side of Bob Jones proved that he was ahead of his time. The music industry needed good security to not only look after the band and acts but the punters as well. We learned that the acts didn't want heavy handed security. It was becoming close-knit where the security were not only bodyguards to the band but integrated along with them. They could hold up a conversation, fit on the seat in economy, take there wife shopping and keep them fit and trained. There was a new wave of security which was taking off where Bob Jones and Richard Norton had established. I was soon to find out that if it wasn't for the legendary hard-core rock and roll image that Jimmy Barnes carved from being front man of Cold Chisel to entering a successful solo career, I may have still been fighting my way through the countdown at the Thornlie.

## No Comment

As the style was growing, Rod and I were confronted with more and more people wanting to work in with us or work against us. We had taken over many security contracts for pubs, clubs and concerts. We already had a reputation in Perth, and along with that dealing with enemies and bullies. Paul Moyle trained in Rod's Dojo, became a 3rd Dan and one of the instructors in the club. However, he would hit white belts with flying sidekicks till they bounced off the walls. Rod kept warning him to lay off the beginners as this was not part of the Zen Do Kai teachings. It was a challenge to keep a hold of every single person in the organisation and he was one of them. At our black belt classes, I was the enforcer and tuned Paul up a few times. I suppose he didn't accept this and ended up changing styles. I thought, good riddens, he was a bully anyway. I was to find out this was not the end. He started working and training alongside Brian Mackie, who was the competition and well known in Perth. I was glad that he left Zen Do Kai as one bad apple can send the wrong message to students just starting out. He could deter people from wanting to learn Martial Arts. This was not enough for him, we started hearing through the grapevine he was also bad-mouthing us. Call us a dog and we will bite your head off like one.

Barnesy was in town and he rented a Ford LTD. It was October 1983, Jimmy was touring with Cold Chisel, and so we took him out for a drink at the Leederville Hotel. Our ears were still ringing from "Khe Sanh" and low and behold, who is working on the door? Paul Moyle along with another doorman we knew as, "Big Maori Mick" words were exchanged, and a bit of push and shove. Paul scurried out the back door with his tail between his legs. As they say in the school yard, don't dish it out if you can't take it. When we left for the night, Jimmy's rented LTD was stolen. We never found out who stole it, but there was a cop in the crowd who saw the altercation and would be a witness in a case against me that Paul took years to pursue.

Rod and I were walking in the main street mall in Perth CBD. We noticed a couple of beat cops walking beside us and wondered if they were following us. As eight uniformed police began surrounding us, I was just as confused as the police. They surrounded us and said we want to talk to you. They began telling me about some warrant but they were not very specific and had no paper work whatsoever. So I knew at this stage what my rights were and kept on walking. They kept following us and Rod kept asking "What are you charging him with?" They couldn't answer so we kept walking. In fact, I started feeling paranoid as they followed us through traffic lights and city crosswalks. Why was I being pursued on the street? If they had a warrant, wouldn't they come knocking on the door? I later found out they didn't have a last known address. We started to draw a crowd and I'm sure some people thought we robbed a bank. They were clearly frustrated and started to grab me by the arm. They must not have read our profile beforehand. Noel Watson, brash, will not cooperate, a.k.a. Noel Quarrel. Rod Stroud, bush lawyer, also will not cooperate. Rod kept palming their hands off me. "If you're not arresting or charging him, where going." he persisted. By now, the cops surrounding us multiplied by twenty. Finally, the CIB arrested me and bundled me in the back seat with a cop on each side. Here I go again flanked by clowns. When I got in the back of the car they tried to intimidate me saying they were going to take me to the outskirts of Perth and tune me up. I said "yeah no worries do your best." When I got to the Mount Lawley police station, I could tell they had it in for me. Typical mannerisms such as you know we know this person and so on and so on, I knew I was being railroaded in the land of the kangaroo courts. In 1984, I was charged with assault on Paul Moyle. I asked Evan Kakulas to represent me. He kept saying he was not a criminal lawyer but a family lawyer. I insisted that I was not a criminal and that I wanted him to be my lawyer. Even though I lost the case, I thanked Evan for trying to help me anyway. Not long after that something good happened to me. I went to Cold Chisel's 'Last Stand'. It was Chisel's farewell concert, held at the Sydney Entertainment Centre. At the time, it was huge that this legendary rock band was breaking up. I stayed with Jimmy at his hotel and the next day Jim, Jane and I went up to Bowral to look at a 2 bedroom cottage that he was going to purchase. He wanted to move his family away from the city life and from all the hassles of drunken fans roaming around his house. His car got stolen 3 times and with Mahalia just a baby he was concerned for her and Jane. He asked me again to move over to Sydney and look after them full time. I knew I couldn't leave Genghis, but I agreed to tour with him and teach him karate. We finished the day with the best 'beetroot and cheese' sandwich at this small cafe in Bowral. Life is looking good.

I had been on and off the road for nearly five years. I was unaware of the outstanding criminal injury charge that Paul Moyle was pursuing against me. Usually, it is posted in the newspaper and if you miss it, they automatically award the victim. The West Australian newspaper posted a public notice in 1988 where there was some doubt whether I received the notice. I felt it was an injustice as I had not shown up for the hearing and neither did Mr Rat Moyle as he now resided interstate. He lied all over his statement saying he was a barman, not a bouncer and that he could no longer work in the industry anymore. He lied about a few other things just to railroad me as he was now practising to become a lawyer. He had a previous eye infection and tried to get the magistrate to award him with injuries received by us. He also went on the dole and collected unemployment lying to the government that he could not work in the hospitality industry for fear of retribution. His assessment for injuries received was for the sum of $3,500. I was sent a four page assessment every few months and would complete all the necessary financial requirements. After about a year, I decided to pay the whole thing off figuring once I got rid of this debt, it would be out of my mind forever. My hand writing scrolled out on the bottom of the page. I am on medication...but I am getting much better with time. It was appropriately signed using spaghetti sauce or ketchup. Rod suggested rather than payable to 'Town Clerk', that I make the cheque out to 'Town Jerk'. Genghis would help me lick the stamp, so by the time it left my house it was dripping.

In the land of kangaroo courts, I learned huge lessons if ever to face the justice system again. Like going into battle, prepare for your court case as much as possible, do your own homework and don't drink water from the glass in the courtroom. This would often be an admission of guilt. Evan Kakula's family owned a great deli on a corner street in Northbridge. On occasional visits for salami or nuts, he would say, "Noel, let me know if you ever want to get divorced."

*Retro Photos of the Boys and Genghis*

*Jim, Swannie and Genghis playing with nunchakus. Rod, Jim & I*
*on X-mas day in Bowral. Jim and Wayne Gardner.*

## Samurai swordplay

SHADES of Shogun in Perth? The senjoists (they're a group of martial artists) put on a glittering display of Japanese costumes and weapons used in this ancient Japanese art. The costumes are similar to those worn by battlers in the samurai movie, Shogun. The sword wielded by Rod Stroud is worth more than $6000 and Noel Watson, in red, is the guy trying to get out of the way.

*Rod just a cut above Noel*

# CHAPTER 5

# Crazy Noel on the Road

Being thought of as a violent crazy person has advantages as well as disadvantages. On the plus side people, particularly those who may want to mess with you will have second thoughts. On the negative side it does not do much for your employability. Even if you are the best security guard in the world, with a nickname like "Crazy Noel" club owners will make sure you spend most of your time where they can keep an eye on you; standing on the outside entrance of run down clubs that smell of beer and stale chips to scare people into behaving. That's because the owners want peace in their establishments not blokes sent packing through plate glass windows. That's bad for business and no one wants their insurance premiums going up. So you stand for hours making sure nothing happens. It's usually boring, mundane, doesn't pay well and often (because we are outside at night) a bone chilling way to making a living. As "Crazy Noel" that was the career path I was heading for. However, I have to say that at this point in my life I was light years ahead of where I ever thought I'd be. Working with my best mate Rod in Perth for Bob Jones, I wasn't on the dole. I was making a respectable wage and for the first time in my entire life had money in my pocket at the end of the week. For someone who grew up with cardboard in his shoes so the holes wouldn't show and who spent his early days standing outside bakeries, smelling the fresh bread and wishing he could one day eat a cream bun instead of weetbix and vegemite, it was nothing short of a miracle. Making $15 as hour was such an unusual thing in my life, it made me feel rich. Granted it wasn't what Mum would've wanted for me. As far as she and most of my mates in Brisbane were concerned. I was 'Crazy Noel' a guy who worked on the door because he didn't have any education or trade. The odd thing is it was a trade. It was not just the karate and street fighting that I picked up but how to manage crowds and to make people do what I wanted without having to hurt anybody. This is not to say that it was an easy job. Walking into dark clubs spotting trouble makers several days a week and saying politely, "Sorry mate, you've abused your privileges in this club, you're not welcome here now" (that would always get them) and then waiting for the reaction which inevitably on cue was that the person would turn red with anger, shape up, call me or Rod a wanker then start punching. You throw them out with limited display of force. A little bit of street theatre. No one really gets hurt except for a bruised ego and then business as usual. I never really wanted to hurt anybody or cause a fight for the sake of fighting. Being a show off was not part of the code. It's not like the movies where you always have to show you are tough. In the security business you're assumed to be a bit tough or you wouldn't be doing it. For the most part guys in the bars were not dangerous. They were usually big talkers, not trained, bigger than they were smarter, with no real appetite for a fight they couldn't win by bashing someone smaller in 15 seconds. The ones we learned to watch for were the street fighter. They were the quiet ones at the edge of the crowd. Good posture, balanced on their feet and a serious intimidating animal look in their eyes that liked the adrenalin rush of a serious fight. This was their drug. Big or small these guys would fight to death and you have to make sure that as a doorman for the club that didn't happen. Street fighting is not anything you can learn in a karate school. There are no half fights in street fighting. No threats, no talking, no waiting for someone to make the next move. No strategic-like thinking, I will move on his inside so he'll be off balance. It is hell for leather with fists, knives, broken glass, baseball bats, brass knuckles and sometimes anything handy. So fast there isn't time to think and the only way to win is to have trained so hard you can fight so fast that your instincts and reflexes cause the guys you are fighting to fall down and feel enough pain to stop.

## Working with Jimmy Barnes

I rang Malcolm Anderson, who ran Bob Jones Corp. in Queensland and also owned Blood Axe Kennels for a Rottweiler pup. "Send me one with the biggest head; I'll name him Genghis Khan".

Cold Chisel just happened to be on the same flight. I picked up Jimmy Barnes first and we went over to the cargo to fetch my 5-week old pup. The guy at the cargo told me Genghis had chewed through the plastic cage and was nipping at the greyhound paw next to him. Great we'll have a big party and initiate Genghis into the world of Rock and Roll. The band showed up and shook his paw to thank him for the invite.

It was shortly after this that Cold Chisel broke up in 1983. Jimmy went straight on the road. He was a hard-working singer. In fact, during this time Australian bands were some of the hardest working bands in the world. This was how they made it. Jimmy was no different. He toured everywhere. The owners would usually pack the live pub shows. The fire and licensing were fairly unregulated back then. Security was changing and Jimmy wanted to make sure that the punters were not only getting their money's worth for the show but that they were safe as well. As a security coordinator, I met with the in-house security prior to the shows. This would mainly take place while the band did sound check. If I knew the pubs were very rough, I could always find a couple of Zen Do Kai security to attend to backstage. It never failed, even in country towns of New Zealand, they were always available. It also helped that a few of the boys were on the guest list. Jimmy was always very generous with backstage passes and autographed posters. The Odin's Warriors Motorcycle Club did the security at the Beenleigh. I always found them to be very professional and not heavy-handed. Normally, the stadium shows had 8-10 security working the pit. I would usually hire 6-8 security just to do backstage. We needed to provide an area near the front for Jimmy's disabled fans, which we closed off and protected from the rest of the crowd. We always double checked the perimeter of the front stage ensuring that any sharp corners were gaffa-taped up. Before going on stage, I scanned the outside to see if anyone was selling any boot-leg merchandise. Once all the checks were done, I would find a place to do a work out with Jimmy before the show. The photographers were given the first three songs to take their shots. During the shows, I stood close to right of stage where I could clearly see Jimmy and the crowd. This was to ensure the safety from flying objects and overzealous fans jumping on stage. Of course, Barnesy was not your average artist. One of his favourite things to do was to jump into the pit. On one occasion, the crowd parted leaving him with eight stitches. The punters were also closely watched that they were not overcome by the heat. The security working in the pit was responsible for spraying water bottles to the crowd. If a punter looked overwhelmed, the guys usually pulled them off to the side and called the paramedics if needed.

Beneath all of these towns that seem so quiet on the surface there is a smoking volcano waiting to explode. Jimmy was evolving in his music. He was constantly scouting new talent for support bands or musicians for his own band. As Jimmy's popularity grew so too the need for security. I appreciated this as security seemed to be the last thing people thought about when running clubs. Rod and I were usually outnumbered, which is what probably kept us afloat. Touring with Jimmy, I began to see familiar faces in each town. I knew that most of the nightclubs or pubs where Jim played, the security were either Zen Do Kai or one of the boys. This made our job a lot easier. I think Jimmy knew he could count on us, especially through the red dust rough towns. Usually, Rod would take care of the band and I could concentrate on Jimmy and the family. It was funny to see the band running to the car that Jimmy and I were going to be in, pleading if they could come with us. Rod was not afraid to speed through those towns with the bands scared shitless.

Soon after Jimmy went solo, he wanted to become more focused and disciplined and was interested in the spiritual side of martial arts. Jane Barnes encouraged more of this discipline as well. He felt his training helped his breathing especially as a singer. He had road crew, band members and many times his young family. When Cold Chisel toured they didn't use security they had hard core road crew who played the dual role. Jimmy was now running a big business and it was at this time he was also looking again at the American market. The unsuccessful attempt with Chisel was still fresh in his mind. When he came to Perth he thanked me for all the free drinks I supplied whenever he toured with Chisel. We were running most of the pubs and clubs so it was always mate's rates. Jimmy asked me to go on tour with him full time security, training and travel companion. We did a small tour before heading to America. I trained him as much as he had time to commit to Martial Arts. We opened for ZZ Top in the states while Jimmy was promoting his album. The Canadian management were always questioning Jimmy about everything. This is the music business. We were at the office of Bruce Allen and Jimmy was in a meeting. He came out and said "Noel, they want to have a chat". I could see a cheeky smirk and wondered what do these guys want to talk to me about? I sat down in front of this large music promoter as he started to fire away with the questions. "What is your role here?"

"Why are you here?" At this stage it was just Jimmy and I. Mark Pope and Richard Macdonald, Jimmy's managers had not arrived. I could sense their vibe, and I was not happy. Why should I have to justify to them. I was working for Jimmy. If they didn't know why I was there, they would soon find out. I glared at him and the only thing I was thinking was to grab him and pull him over the desk. I had flash backs of what I did to my neighbour. Instead, I told them "Fine, get rid of me, you try keep Jimmy focused. As a 5th dan you are taught about containment or the ninja art of concealment. I was always in battle mode and favoured the red side of the Senjo. If I wanted to be a professional bodyguard and rid myself of the "Crazy Noel" image I would have to gravitate towards the blue side or at least the yellow side which is somewhere between the middle ground. I walked out of the room and saw a punching bag in the corner of the office. Like Chisel, I thought about that song, "you got nothing I want, you got nothing I need." Jimmy waited outside with that cheeky grin. I think he was waiting to hear some racket or me pulling him over the desk giving him a grease and oil change. I didn't want any dramas and thought I would be out of here. Obviously, they underestimated the loyalty we had built up. Jimmy said, "If you go I'm going too." Instead, he got me blind drunk and when the security wanted to kick me out, this time Jimmy was the bodyguard and I was the singer. "You might get him out, but you may lose an eye." He said to the bouncers. That night Jimmy's son Jackie was born. He told Jackie that when we celebrated that night I was more excited than him.

As the tour progressed they began to see that the training helped Jimmy's stamina on the road. I was extra tough on him, no rock star treatment here. There was a misconception that your friend is your instructor and you'll get it easy. He kept up with whatever I dished out. Even though, he partied hard he still kept up with me on the running. There weren't a lot of choices in the arena to train, just concrete blocks with road crew setting up. You get adventurous and there is nothing better than a shower block for push-ups and sit-ups. Jimmy started to thrive on it just like singing he flourished under pressure. Looking at his hands he started to build up callouses on his knuckles. In martial arts this becomes your point of contact, they eventually become hammer-like.

## Looking for Huckleberry Finn

We caught a cab to a bar in New Orleans, the driver overheard our Scottish and Australian accents, when he pulled over he told us he had something to sell. He opened the back boot and showed us an arsenal of weapons. We quickly declined and mentioned we were not very good on the drink and might end up shooting each other. We were both well and truly under way at this bar. I went to the loo and when I got back, Jimmy was outside surrounded by all the bouncers who chucked him out. They quickly threw me out alongside him. "C'mon, let's get em!" Jimmy says. "Jim, there are times to be a samurai and times not to be and this is it. So off we went to the next bar for more drinks. "We're just looking for Huckleberry Finn?!" the locals thought we were not only drunk and boisterous but from another world. We came across some higher ranking officials. "Don't know what nationality you are (pointing the finger at Jim) but you and your Aussie mate better get out of this town or else?!" We went back to the hotel and Jimmy rang Jane. He fell asleep on the phone and when he woke up his bill was $1000!

## The Tour Bus

If you bottle up a samurai on a bus from 10pm to 6am trying to catch some sleep smelling everyone's shoes and unable to do number 2's on the bus you sometimes start to lose it. That's why I was looking forward to Jane and the family coming on tour as much as Jimmy. I knew Jane would give the management a serving for making me feel unwelcome and uncomfortable. When the bus pulled up it had "Crazy Horse" on the front sign. Jimmy wanted his own bus too. We were all away from home and in a different place every night. The bus driver was a professional wrestler from the South and we got along well. He was the only one who could put up with Jimmy on the walkie-talkie all night calling the other truckies 'red necks' and looking for 'midget hookers'.

I started to feel more at home and at peace with the lifestyle besides the truck stop food this is where I got a taste of exciting food. Jimmy and Jane were both very competent cooks. Where ever we went Jimmy and Jane would seek the best Thai, Chinese or Japanese restaurant in town. Besides your usual bacon and eggs, soup with crackers, the truck stops were a form of entertainment for me. You could find a large range of fireworks and one in particular had rows of martial arts equipment such as ninja stars, nunchakus and samurai swords.

# Samurai Skiing and Peabody Ducks

Jimmy wasn't going to forget the gruelling training sessions and it was payback time. He took us skiing to Grouse Mountains in Canada and paid for a quick lesson. He whisked me away to the professional slope because he knew I had never skied before. He knew I couldn't back down. At this point I only knew how to snow plough and whatever I had seen on Wide World of Sports. "Follow me!" he yells. I was flying down this mountain through moguls and desperately trying to stay up. I was thinking if I make it down in one piece Jimmy is dead meat! I see him at the bottom of the slope eating snow with laughter. Jimmy knew that skiers lean forward off the centre of balance and martial artist were used to standing in the centre of balance. I'm sure he wanted to get me out of my element. After a few more times I start to get the hang of it. In between we headed to the bar to drink beer with vitamin B. This seems to help when we ski at night. Jimmy and Jane were fun to hang with. They called us "The Griswolds" as we were always venturing off taking the kids to theme parks to break up the monotony on tour. We stayed at the famous Peabody Hotel. It is well known for the resident ducks that play in the pond. I thought what a great idea a splash pool in the middle of the hotel lobby. I jumped in and the management were totally flabbergasted. The pond was for the ducks not some crazy Australian! ZZ Top organized the private tour of 'Graceland' I followed the strict instructions to 'Keep off the Grass'.

# A Night in Newcastle

I am used to teaching Jimmy Barnes karate. I punch him. He punches me back. We train. I hit him hard. He hits me harder it gets the blood rushing through our bodies and gets me focused. He head butted me once and chipped my tooth. Thinking he would be dead meat, he recommended his dentist that does white fillings.

By now most of the band is accustomed to country towns. Tonight we are in Newcastle. It is a steel town and working class to the core. This is no place to be careless. Everyone in the business knows that the crowd here rioted at the closing of the famous "Star Hotel". Cars were burnt, police were bashed. The riot made such an impression that it inspired Don Walker of "Cold Chisel" to write one of their best-selling songs "Star Hotel". Rod and I have learned the hard way that it is better to avoid trouble in the first place than turn a regional tour of country towns into a "Mad Max" experience. So tonight I am telling everyone in Jimmy's crew to pay attention and mind their manners as they walk through the crowd. The gig goes off without any major hiccups except when we are leaving. One of the keys to controlling these kinds of situations is making sure that the cars are parked in the right direction and that everybody has an exit strategy. I advise all the members of the band to keep their windows up and the doors locked and to always remember that at the end of the night there are going to be a lot of young hyped-up lads looking for a little excitement. The fans at Jimmy's shows congregate at the end of the car park trying to get a last look at Jimmy as we pull out. As usual he is amped to the tilt. Jane is not with us tonight so to prepare Jimmy for the four hour ride home I have packed a couple bottles of Stolichnaya Vodka, 4 litres of lemonade, a nicely cut lime and a bucket of ice. This is just part of the service of a bodyguard making sure that every detail is taken care of. Upon leaving the venue I see a guy reach in and grab the hair of lead guitarist Jeff Neil, who is in the car ahead of us with the record execs who have come for the show. All the training we've been doing, it was only natural for Jimmy to leap out of the car and give me a hand. I have to be faster than Jimmy now and on my toes, so I quickly catch up to the guy grab him from behind, spin him around and give him a quick jab.(bang, bang, bang in and out) The record execs are stunned that everything happened so fast it was like an action scene. When I look back and think about it, this is what this lifestyle does. I am constantly looking, feeling and breathing for trouble or confrontation. The combination of being on the road in the pubs and nightclub environments builds up to an almost automatic reaction. Most of Jimmy's hard-core fans are well behaved and meet us in every town or show. They have a common respect for each other and save spots at the front of stage. I got to know most of them and Jimmy joked one night how I even had a fan club.

## Back to Bowral

Like a shark-toothed ghost, the hire car glides effortlessly through quaint antique shops and high class cafes once we hit Bowral. It is night and day from the world I come from. I never drank coffee before I started to work with Jimmy. So I skull a couple of coffee's for the night drive home. It's about 2 am and I am having flashbacks of a journalist we had in the back seat after leaving a gig in Lismore on the way back to the Gold Coast. He described Jimmy and me as a pair of outlaws escaping from jail. The music was blaring full blast from the sound system and Jimmy was drinking to unwind. Winding down after a gig is a little like prepping in the restaurant business. It's a ritual you have to do. Jimmy kept the music so loud I used to plug my ears with toilet tissues. In the meantime my foot is flat chat to the floor and we are making time as we head for home. The CD player is playing some of Jimmy's favourites', AC/DC, Def Leppard and Prince. We are making good timing as we barrel through the night. Jimmy is bopping around like a boxer after a fight. He likes to grab my ears and head butts me, while putting a few jabs into the sides of my head. For him I make allowances. I know that the next day when Jimmy is training with me I make sure he pays. Suddenly Jimmy pulls the hand brake up! The car starts to skid out of control and Jimmy is laughing like crazy! Only one thing to do to keep control I reach over and elbow him hard. More laughter as he is totally oblivious to the pain. By 4:30am it's getting cold and by 5 am the night is crystal clear. One by one I pass huge trucks shipping steel. Weaving in and out I feel as if I have put 20 cents in a video slot. I glance over at Jimmy and see that his hair is standing straight up. Just before dawn, when the wombats are out I am hoping to reach Bowral without feeling the impact of a huge furry animal on my teeth as it smashes against the front of the car. At last we reach Bowral and make for Jimmy's property. It is dawn and freezing. The road is covered in fog so dense that it forces me to put the bright lights on. As I come to a stop he jumps out of the car grabs an axe and starts chopping wood. He's says he's chopping wood for the fire to make me warm when we get inside. I see the axe head flying and I am just as worried he is going to chop up his fully restored 1948 pickup truck as he brings down the axe again and again. "That's all right Jim I say after a while. Let's go in." We walk into the huge house and he picks one of the rooms. "This one good for you?" he asks. "Yeah, mate, fine" Then he notices the bed is not made and the doona has no cover. He gets the sheets and says "Now I'm going to teach you something!" He carefully demonstrates how to put the doona cover over the bed spread. It is a meticulous task. You have to place the two end bits inside and keep shaking until the sheet is completely covered. Jimmy Barnes rock star is also Jimmy Barnes expert in comforters.

## End of the Road and other Antics

Tony Brock (who was the drummer for Rod Stewart), Jimmy and I were driving from Perth to Geraldton in Western Australia. This guy kept following along trying to run us off the road. He would speed up after us, pull in front and slow down. This was beginning to escalate each time I tried to get away. I tried to let him pass again and he tried to run us off the road. By the third time, I tried to pass he pulled over. This time I stopped too and Jimmy and Tony ran out of the car towards him. I quickly panicked and approached the 4-wheel drive with some caution. My first thoughts were I better get to this guy before Jimmy does. "Mate, what the fuck are you doing?? Trying to run us off the road?" He was a big country bloke. Just before he grabbed me in through the window, I head butt him with everything I had. I start to lay a couple of punches on him.

I figure his hands are too busy. He is out cold, slumped over the steering wheel. I look up and see Jimmy and Tony, eyes wide open with a cheeky grin. "He'll be fine." I said, "We better go don't wanna be late" I get into the car with the posse and Jimmy turns up the music. "Welcome to Western Australia! Jimmy wails". I will be your friendly tour guide. After the gig, we head back to Perth another 5 hours on the road. It is the same posse Tony, Jimmy and I. This time I take a wrong turn, we are lost in the middle of nowhere, running out of gas and freezing our arses off. I have no idea where we are. "How can you be lost?" says Jim. "Aren't you from Perth?" "Go knock on the door of that house!" says Jim "You go and knock, I'm pretty sure they'll let you in. You're the rock star." It's 4am do you really think they will get up? He grins but goes and knocks anyway.

"No one is answering, he says, we'll have to build a fire and maybe sleep here for the night." Great, it's not like we are camping, just vodka, lime, lemonade, a few CD's and a couple of enthusiastic rock stars. I finally say lets' just keep going until we have to stop. Thank goodness, someone was feeling sorry for me, just a few miles up the road and we see an open petrol station.

Jimmy wasn't always blasting music. On some of the long country drives, he would lay down in the back seat listening to audio tapes about Sherlock Holmes, Mozart and Ned Kelly. This was relaxing for both of us especially if Jimmy was hung over, but he'd always pop his head up and say, "You right mate?" We'd look forward to the next truck stop and the traditional Bacon and Egg burger with barbeque sauce.

Jimmy was a prankster and often came up with creative ways to kill time. He used to get up to some wild things when he was with Cold Chisel. If they were pissed off with the hotel management, they'd leave prawns and fish in the roof cavity. The Cold Chisel shows taught us literally about being on your toes. By now we are used to Jimmy's antics on stage, the crowd jumping, the stage jumping, and the running through the crowd like a mad-man. Before the cordless microphones were invented we were constantly following up the cord during the entire show. The crowd used to get tangled up and we sometimes could not keep up the pace. Although he calmed a bit when he went solo, we once frantically tried to get him out of the pit. He emerged back on stage with a small piece of fabric left hanging from his collar. He yelled out, "For fuck sake, I just bought that shirt today cost me heaps!" When his bushido cross got ripped off his neck, he shouted out to the crowd it had gone missing and the next day it was returned. Rod and I often thought about getting full-faced helmets.

Johnny Diesel joined us for a few of the tours and Jimmy used to get him that drunk we'd wheel him into the hotel using a stand up trolley. Then Jimmy organized someone to put all the furniture (including the bed) stacked up in the bathroom. I often wondered how he creatively came up with these pranks. He took all the light bulbs out and placed one of those battery-operated barking dogs. When Diesel arrived back in his room he tied his suitcase to the back of the door with a rope over the balcony. Jimmy had strict instructions for me. Don't play any tricks, don't give Noel any drugs and don't give him strong drinks. He must have thought I didn't have a sense of humour. Once we were all drinking in the hotel bar. I refused to drink anymore and went upstairs to bed. Jimmy shouted everyone drinks in the bar and billed my room! Tony and Jimmy were always playing up. We were in Coffs Harbour and they played golf in the room. There were holes all over the place. I heard the huge bangs coming through the room and wondered what that was. I see them dressed in raincoats, the spa bath filled with water and they are happy playing golf!

When the tour was wrapping up we would often do a couple of shows in New Zealand. I talk about the smoking volcano ready to erupt. This is it. The fans are just as wild. The tour buses have sheep skin seat covers and the crowd usually chants... Baaa..rnsey.... Baaa... rnsey.... Baaa... rnsey like a herd of sheep. Some of the band from Canada were not accustomed to New Zealand or specifically the hard-core fans. The promoter, a respected elder is also the leader of one of the many Maori gangs. He invites Jimmy and the crew to a traditional 'hangi'. We stop at the house where the party is and make our way to the back yard. We see about 300 gang members in their colours, some fully tattooed. The vibe is powerful and still. We stand quietly in front while they do the 'haka'. It was impressive to experience their culture. Of course, as part of the tradition each member rubs noses with you. I could tell the band were nervous and shy. They didn't want to upset anyone as they tried to remember what to do. Peter Kekel mucked up a few times as he looked to Jimmy and me in desperation. We are asked back into the house for some lunch. The band follows Jimmy and me single file into the house. We sit down and it is traditional for the guest to eat first. Nobody says a word and just eats. They invite us to the Clubhouse for a drink. As we head off to their clubhouse Jimmy says to everyone, "Whatever you do, let them win at pool."

By the summer of '86, it seems as though the touring has not stopped. We were not only touring full-on with Jimmy, The Australian Made concerts were taking off in every state. We toured alongside INXS, Models, Divinyls, The Saints, I'm Talking, The Triffids and Mental as Anything. This was a fun tour; the plane was full of rock stars and pranksters. Michael Hutchence would get on the plane wearing board shorts, cowboy boots, Kurubra hat and overcoat and still manage to pull the look off. Jane and I were always saying how he could look good in a garbage bag. We were all given free pairs of shoes from Reebok. When the airline stewardess did the safety features demonstration, we would hang our shoes by the laces all at the same time, in front of our faces to demonstrate the oxygen mask. By the time Australian made came around Rod and I helped to secure more business for Zen Do Kai. This gave Bob Jones Corporation a larger profile. Some of our other mates from Zen Do Kai were already working alongside some of the international acts. Noel Rush was working as Billy Joel's full-time security; Tony Quinn was working for the Eurhythmics and Gary Pettersen for UB40 and Simple Minds.

## Stray Cat Strut

One band that I took a liking to were the Stray Cats. In the early 80's, we had done venue security for them in one of the old Perth Theatres. At this stage in the USA they were opening for the Rolling Stones and carving a huge market in the Rockabilly Scene. Ten years later they were still as dynamic as ever with their stripped down production and lighting. For a three piece band, the music really spoke for itself. They opened some of the shows in New Zealand for Jimmy Barnes and we got to know them real well. Brian Setzer and Jimmy Barnes sang "Little Darling". Slim Jim started working out with me, punching and kicking the pads and he too had that uncanny evil eye so we got on like a house on fire. The Stray Cats grew up in Queen's New York on the hard side of the tracks so I was quite at ease knowing we had similar type backgrounds. Slim Jim's Dad was a NY fireman and would enter booby trapped buildings raging with fire. I think they are the true warriors in life. At the time, he was married to Britt Ekland, whom I remembered as only seeing in the James Bond movies. All of their wives were so friendly and gracious. The management asked me to do security for their Japan tour which would end its last leg in Australia. When dealing with Eric Gardner and Stuart Ross, this level of management were so professional with briefcases and equipment on wheels. They even explained that it wasn't 24/7 security, just take the boys where ever they wanted to go. For the Stray Cats, they were happy to play Pinball in the Arcade. I was used to seeing the Howard Freeman type management with Dragon where they would drive Mini Mokes into the hotel pool. However, working with different bands and touring is another form of gang trust. Loyalty, hanging with your own kind it is rare for outsiders to get into the inner circle. That's why I too couldn't work with just anybody. You have to know when to talk, listen and when to observe. You also have to have a personality and be able to blend in and be another band member.

It's a few hours from the airport to our hotel in Tokyo and I realize the band is all getting in at different times. So I spend the first day going back and forth to the airport until all three were settled in. I woke up fresh and head towards the hotel gym for a vigorous workout. It feels a bit different to working with Jimmy, as I have to pace myself and would sometimes be driving back to Bowral or just getting in from the nightclubs. I run into Brian Setzer and he tells me, "I can't go to the pool because of all my tattoos." It's a Yakuza thing. I thought similar to Red Hill Boys; Yakuza's get profiled as well. I know it is a way of life in Japan and usually you don't have to worry unless you travel around in those circles. The closer to the interior we toured, I could sense the young Yakuza energy. Most of my daytime hours would be spent with Brian. He was the most recognized Stray Cat and could not walk a few steps from the hotel without being mobbed. The rockabilly scene was huge in Harajuku, 40 bands all lined up in the street playing at the same time. Shops full of Rock and Roll merchandise. The Beatles, The Rolling Stones, Elvis Presley and even the Stray Cats had their own store. The Japanese fans are quite different though, I only had to put my hand up in a criss-cross motion and on cue they would politely step back with such grace and respect. Even Bobby Gilken, the drum tech would tell me that the promoter had an interpreter there at all times and would listen attentively when setting things up. They only had to show them once and everything would be in the exact order. The promoters were well organized and I almost felt guilty as how easy everything was. Soba Noodles at the same place that I saw in Black Rain, dinners at these amazing Japanese restaurants, and a John Lennon watch given to me by the record company. Japan gave me such inspiration for street-vendor type food. I knew that Nagoya was famous for its chicken wings and thought, such an easy concept, I bet he's making a million dollars.

Once the sun goes down and we get ready for the gigs, nothing is left to chance. I visit all three rooms and pick up Brian, Slim Jim and Lee; we head to the lift together. Rockabilly hair-do's, studded leather jackets and pointy shoes, the lift opens and we see Akebone, one of the most popular sumo wrestlers who is from Hawaii and his two top hat security. The elevator is not that big but instead of waiting for the next one, I immediately decide that we can all squeeze in together. We all take two to three cautious steps to what is left of the elevator space, and slowly pivot our backs to them. It's a moment in time that you sometimes never forget. When all is silent and somewhat awkward as you stop to listen to your own thinking, worried that they actually know what you are thinking. When we get down to the hotel lobby, the rest of Akebone's crew are waiting. Mixed in with some of the Rockabilly fans, it looks like a movie set. I see parked on the street the most unusual looking Harley-Davidson motorcycle I have ever seen. All the paint had been completely grinded off. I wondered who owned this rustic and cool looking bike. When we got to the gig, I was checking the perimeter of front stage and the security pulled out this velvet rope across as a barrier. I kept thinking, you are kidding right? Is that it? To my amazement, no one ever crossed that velvet rope. What a gig I thought, sure beats "Gobbles." One of the fans in Kawasaki was taking a photo and the Japanese security started slapping him up. I think it must have been that it was not within the timeframe of which was allowed. I quickly went over to explain, that it was okay, not to worry. The young fans were jumping up and down and the floor collapsed. When we went back to that same venue the next tour there was a sign, "NO JUMPING." After the gig, we were driven back to the hotel; I started noticing that all of the drivers wore white gloves. I thought this was quite unusual, even if it wasn't a limousine. You also spend a lot of time looking out of windows. This is especially true in limousines where you are facing each other. We notice this maniacal motorcyclist flying down the highway at 100 miles an hour. I take a closer look and it is that grinded down rustic Harley that was parked out the front of the hotel. He must have been such a huge fan of the Stray Cats. He was literally risking his life trying to snap a photo laughing and yelling out without a care in the world. Just enjoying the moment of being an insane paparazzi!

We arrive back in Australia for the next leg of the tour. I enjoyed my time in Japan, especially because the band were easy, I got along with all the management and I got to see one of the melon heads, Shaun Keating. We went drinking one night in a Karaoke bar and he spent the night in my room on the floor. I played a trick on him and stuffed newspaper in his shoes. He only realized half way down the street why his toes were cramping up.

After one of the shows in Melbourne, we arrive back at the hotel and I spot a huge rockabilly Cadillac downstairs. The hotel lobby is full of Rockabilly fans but it doesn't consume me because I know they are all very respectable. The boys sign a few autographs and head up the lift to disperse to their rooms. By now, I know everyone's routines, during the day Brian asks me to take him where he can have a pork roll with brown gravy and we usually meet at the hotel bar after the gig. Slim Jim will usually join Brian and me whilst Lee usually stays up in his room. I get to my room and gravitate towards the window again, do some breathing and light stretches and check out what is happening on the street. I am always superstitious about sitting on the bed. My mate Steve Fyfield always told me that this is usually the first thing they do in jail. Sit or lie in the bed looking up at the ceiling for 23 hours in the day. So I decide to sit quietly in Moksha, palms up and remove distracting thoughts, but I sense the night is not over. An hour passes, and the phone rings, it's Lee and he wants to get a bite to eat. "Sure mate, I'll come down to your room." There was never any awkwardness with the Stray Cats, spending time in close proximity you get comfortable as if you have known each other for years and years. Lee was no different, like I, he had karate fingers from playing the double bass. Before the gig, he would coat his fingers with super glue.

When we get to the hotel lobby there are still a few fans, he stops for just a brief moment to sign an autograph, but I gesture to the rest that we have somewhere to go. I still see the Cadillac and wave a goodbye to the heavy-set Rockabilly. I assess the scene ahead and see a group of bouncers arguing with a group of people. I body swerve Lee past and we head further up to the kebab shop in Melbourne's Chinatown. I see another group of guys kicking the hell out of the telephone box, it is about one shop front away from the Kebab shop. I lead Lee inside hoping they don't see us.

I could almost taste the electricity and energy force in the air. The fluorescent lights and the buzzing of the late night crowd immediately felt like a strobe light which can trigger a Norman Bates frenzy. They all enter the kebab shop and immediately start making fun of Lee. His hair, boots, dress sense everything guys would say with piss and bad manners. Lee is just about to order at the counter and they start to push him into the glass sandwich display. I have one advantage I am used to multiple attacks. They jam him from behind again and I spun around to block him and say "Hey... Hey... lay off!" I see the three of them coming at me with fists of rage. I bang the biggest one in the centre with a left lunge jab. I follow up to the guy on the left, with a big over hand right lunge punch to the bridge of the nose, but he whacks me over the head with a crown lager bottle. I was lucky it exploded; otherwise it would have probably cut my head open. The third guy I pivot towards and fang him with a similar left lunge punch. The first three combinations in a street brawl are you're most important. This can also be the deadliest if executed with crispness. The jab to the bridge of the nose not only breaks the cartilage but immediately releases water through your eyes and snaps the brain to the back of the head. These deadly punches can knock someone unconscious. Fully committed lunge punches are difficult to withdraw from. This meaning you need to be able to get back into a cat-stance where you have full control. This will hopefully get you out of a situation. I feel all the bits of glass inside my shirt. No real time to think about anything. All three of them stagger back into the rest of the pack. While Lee and I are pushed even further back in behind the servery. The kebab shop workers are yelling at us for causing havoc in their business, they must be used to seeing this all the time. However, there is nowhere for us to go, if we head out of the shop we get done by the three we just dropped and whoever else was with them. The kebab shop workers push us through the kitchen out the end of the alleyway and shut the door. If they would have let us stay there till the police arrived, perhaps we would have been better off. But they seemed pissed off at us as well. Unfortunately, this was not an option. Where are the cops when I needed them the most? I know I work best under pressure so I try to compose myself, while I quickly think out the exit stragedy. So we make our way to the end of the alley and I know it is not far for Lee to run back to the hotel. He wants to stay but I know it is not his arena and I could not live with myself if he got badly hurt. He hesitates but I say "as soon as we get to the end I want you to run as fast as you can mate, go get some help" I wanted to be certain that Lee would get away without some of them spotting him too. I hear them shout out "there they are!" Lee takes off and all I hear is his (clippity! cloppity! clippity! cloppity!) rockabilly boots moving faster and faster as he bolts back to the end of the street. I think about my options. Option 1, keep on running, no because they will run over the top of both of us and fighting with my back to people has never worked for me. Option 2, end up in the industrial bin with all the leftover Chinese food, or Option 3, go hell for leather and get all over them like a rash. So I spin around and within seconds they are all there. I realize I am going to have to use their brute strength to help me. I am not only outnumbered, but in a life or death situation. These guys mean business if they beat up the telephone box and hit me over the head with a crown lager bottle, what hope do I have? Thinking far ahead can be exhausting, I was right about this; they collected a large piece of wood, the size of a fence paling to make my life even harder. I'm on the balls of my feet, thumbs checking my face and think of 2nd Dan grading. My peripheral vision goes into overload and I know which one is the leader of the pack. He is dressed in black with gold chains and kicking boots. They come at me like a ton of bricks. Nothing too flamboyant as I hit the biggest one with a flying front kick aiming for two feet pass the bodyline, high enough into the solar plexus. I let out the loudest grunt (kiai) ever and he buckles over and vomits. The chunda (vomit) was all over the bottom of my jeans and boots. A kiai is a loud yell that releases energy and blood flow. I rope the dope, grab him in a choke hold and use him as a shield. I hold him as close as I can get and keep feeding it to him, while nutting him on the forehead. Bang! Bang! Oomph! It's fucken survival and I'm just fanging him with all I got. I keep hissing and grunting like a pit bull, I figure this rattles them too. Especially, since he's not feeling to well. He is copping it from his mates who are trying to get to me. They use the fence paling and I hear him grunting with each blow. I'm glad they are not only pissed but a bit stupid too, trying to play baseball with their friends head. But I am starting to run out of gas, thinking I don't know how much longer I can last. Right now it is pure adrenaline. I was getting some clear shots using him as scaffolding as I was able to kick on a 45 degree angle. I could sense the garden bed behind me. How the hell am I going to get out of this one? Then I managed to loosen him up, get one last shot in and toss him into the mix. The next guy throws a half-hearted front kick. I trap catch it, lunge into a deep horse stance and come up to lift his leg straight up and off the centre of balance. This kick which is now braced on my shoulder gets rammed into the bricks. I hear a loud crack as he hits the wall into a perfect concrete sandwich. I cop another blow to the side of the head and start to feel all the glass left in my shirt from the crown lager bottle. I get back on the balls of my feet a second wave of energy is with me. Then, I see some bright lights coming down the alleyway. It is the rockabilly Cadillac! Along with Lee, Slim Jim and Brian are a couple of their rockabilly fans. It was enough of a silhouette to get them off me. So they scattered back, dragged their mates and cowardly take off. They were probably fearful of the heavy-set rockabilly and pointy boots.

When I got back to the hotel, I not only tried picking the glass out of my shirt, but I *reeked*(smelled) of *spew*(vomit) from the guy who vomited on me. Stuart and the Boys suggested I go to the hospital and would provide me with insurance. Of course, I didn't end up going; just a nice long, hot shower and I'll meet you at the bar. It turned into a night of teasing Lee about being the Black Cat. I didn't think so; I think we had good karma that night as it could have been a lot worse. I know the Stray Cats were grateful and it was the red side that worked in my favour. I should've listened to my gut instincts as I pondered out the window and went and got the kebabs myself. Although, we joked that Lee should have ordered room service instead. Every time I see them we always say "Stay away from late night kebab shops and get the pork sandwiches in the day at the local carvery."

When I hear that song "Stray Cat Strut" it reminds me about that night in the alleyway fighting for survival. I'm thankful I had some experience and friends to get me out of that predicament. The Sanchin Kata or Power Kata has the Ibuki breathing, this stems from the 'hara' or lower stomach. When you are deeply emerged in this kata, you develop an enormous amount of power which takes you to a higher level of consciousness. The energy from the ibuki breathing creates power to withstand the pain barrier. The ten sho is the opposite or 'fluid.' When you use this technique or particular Kata it creates immense blood and oxygen to flow gently. When you know how to use both Kata's together, it is Mind, Body and Spirit working and flowing together.

*Jimmy's Big red truck, Rontu fighting with the plastic dinosaur,
Griswold's tour*

*JB in Bowral, Micheal Hutchence, ZZ Top, Tour Bus, Niagara Falls with Barnes Family Jimmy training for his Black Belt*

*Australian Made Tour, London Calling*

*Tin Lids getting ready to tour*

*Noel's Hard passes*

*Stray Cats Autograph*

*Stray Cats Rockabilly's in Japan Tour*

*Slim Jim, Brian Setzer and Lee Rocker*

# CHAPTER 6

# Working on the Rock Pile

When you work as a bouncer or bodyguard, right or wrong you are the protector of oneself as well as others. It never crossed my mind until later that everything I've learned about martial arts has helped me to focus on whatever I was involved with at the time. As far as the philosophical side of martial arts, for me it was more the "Art of War" that intrigued me at most. I was a bit too full-on to sit and be still. In fact, in some aspects writing this book has been a form of lifetime meditation. In "Sun Tzu, The Art of War", many of the philosophies written more than 2000 years ago, and used in the ancient battle strategies can be practiced in business and modern times today. Even in feudal Japan, centuries ago when the samurai ruled the country side they used as much force as necessary to defend their honour. However, the art of the blade was done so with such integrity and etiquette. Once guns were introduced the way of the Bushido was altered forever. When we were younger, we wanted to fight all the time to defend our honour. As we started bouncing, we had to get smarter. Nightclub managers were constantly saying to Rod and I to sort this guy or that guy, they're playing up. We might just as well sort the other 300-400 and be here all night. Can you imagine the Thornlie Hotel with young crazed soccer hooligans? It was similar to going into battle with other countries; Rod and I fighting against England, Ireland and Scotland. Using containment was one of the most difficult issues in dealing with situations as security. When we started doing security everyone seemed anti-security and we were often embroiled in some kind of battle with someone. Nightclub owners and how we ran business, bands and patrons sometimes came down on us if the news media reported on bouncer bashing incidents, other security companies or karate schools and of course, the police if an altercation had occurred. Now you know why they called me Mr Perry, short for Paranoid.

Before we met Jim, his brother Swannie (John Swan) was doing a bit of martial arts. Swannie was one of the original hard-men of rock. He would tell record labels exactly what he thought. I guess we were all the same in our mentality with regard to telling it like it is. Jimmy was and still is a Buddhist and the one thing he liked about the martial arts was that it emphasized self-defence with the least amount of force. You didn't have to beat someone to death. You don't use it as a weapon but as a way of controlling people. Whatever you learn in the four walls of the dojo, will no doubt change once you get into an altercation in the street. Martial arts in the dojo will teach you the fundamentals, but will not guarantee you will come out unscathed. As Bruce Lee always says, work on refining your technique and skills to adapt to your body weight and size, not a one size fits all approach. If you are smaller frame, work on your agility to bridge the gap and deflect from your opponent in a split second. A bulky fighter should work on your technique and speed, knowing you already have the strength factor. If you favour one side of the body, work on the weaker side until it becomes second nature. You learn to strip down to the bare essentials and do what works for you. Teaching Jane Barnes or anyone first learning it is necessary to ensure no contact and self-control. On one of her first lessons she came at me with a fury of fists and kicks like she was headed for the world title. I resorted to a quick click of her heels which swept her off her feet. It is common in teaching circles that white belt women are the easiest to teach because they don't have bad habits and are more likely to have excellent coordination, balance and rhythm. On the other hand, most guys just 'chicken wing' their punches from not having any formal training. A martial artist will have an edge in the self-defence arena because he knows the eight angles of attack, can trigger punch or kick on a 45 degree angle and kick you from anywhere in the octagon. Boxer's like to centre himself and work on bridging the gap. When Jimmy toured in America, we were basically doing up to 3 hours a day. An hour of kata's, weights with push-ups and sit-ups, punching the focus pads and running. "Coming back off the US tour when we got to New Zealand we'd finish up with a couple of hundred kicks. I was the fittest ever in my entire life." says Jim. Initially, he just wanted to get into shape and clear his mind from the hectic schedule. He found that everything worked together. The martial arts gave him stamina to work because on tour you are pre-occupied with the whole thing and all you can think about is the show, travelling and the logistics. Obviously, when you are doing martial arts you are focused on that and your mind clears from thinking about everything else. Meanwhile, you are energized to stay alert and channel your trained energy to concentrate as a performer. When Jimmy was tired half way through the show and felt as if he was losing his concentration, he now had the ability to overcome this barrier. Even if he wasn't 100% fit, he still had the focus and the concentration to maintain his attention.

It takes a lot of courage to walk through the door of a dojo for the first time just as it takes courage to join a gym. As an instructor my approach has always been the same. No matter what your background, if you have the right attitude to learn, you can teach anyone martial arts. The one aspect I emphasize with my students has been awareness. This is even more important than the physical aspect. Your present moment awareness will most likely prevent a situation from even occurring. Working in this industry takes certain sacrifices and can be an occupational hazard. Particularly, in the early hours of the morning when your senses are not only rattled but your nerves are filled with toxic vibrations. Everyone seems to be a practicing lawyer, especially around the universities. Managers and Promoters used to think of security as an after-thought, not within the budget. We knew security as the first and last people you see at the gigs. They changed their approach when tragedy struck and they realized they could lose a fortune.

# Bindoon Rock Festival

At this stage, I had been pretty fortunate to work with most of the top Australian bands. I felt privileged to know and work with the late Michael Hutchence from INXS even before their music career exploded on the International scene. I watched how they grew from a pub barn band in the late 70's to playing regularly at the White Sands and Herdsman Hotel in Perth. In Sydney, Steve Fyfield ran the door at Benny's and the Manzel Room in Kings Cross. These regular haunts and in particular the hotel bar in the Sebel Townhouse is where many bands would meet up between back to back tours, when promoters would schedule the same leg. Wherever I travelled I was almost certain to meet up with Zen Do Kai boys at most night clubs in every capital city including New Zealand. This always meant an endless supply of alcoholic party drinks.

When Jimmy toured, it was not only the regular coastal cities but interior towns as well. Mt. Isa in Queensland, Broken Hill in New South Wales, Bendigo in Victoria, Port Kembla in South Australia, Alice Springs and Darwin in the Northern Territory, Port Headland in Western Australia, and through Tasmania. Cold Chisel, Jimmy and even the Stray Cats had a strong biker following. Western Australia is the land of the fly wave and the wait awhile attitude. Bindoon is about 87 kilometres north of Perth in a tiny little settlement that if you blink you miss the town unless you spot the sign. It is held on a massive property owned by the Coffin Cheaters Motorcycle Club. The festival had been running successfully for about 10 years. Zen Do Kai had always done the security alongside the Coffin Cheaters. The crowd was a good mix of motorcycle enthusiast, clean-skins and hard core fans of rock and roll. Even with the pressure of police and politicians, it was operated with precision and professionalism. No pulling any diva trips at this event. For up and coming young bands it was where they earned their credentials or badge of honour. For seasoned bands like Cold Chisel, Jimmy, Noiseworks and Divinyls it was business as usual. Anything can happen at outdoor gigs and often promoters would rather place in the too hard basket. With such a large road block as the police search every car and motorcycle, any police docket and you're in the paddy wagon back to Perth for high tea with the magistrate. Luckily, we don't get pulled over and slip through a side road slightly before the main entrance. Jimmy is his usual calm before the storm. However, high anxiety will kick in if we pass the hour and a half before the gig. Of course, it doesn't worry me; we are on the same page with this trait. Every band member is well aware of this part of Jimmy's persona. Don't be late, he'll toss you in the crowd and leave you there. Scrooge a familiar face, heavy set marinated biker with terminator shades pulls up next to the car. I roll down the window and the sound of the Harley drowns out the stereo volume even at 54. He reaches his large hand and squeezes my hand till the blood runs dry and says, "Good to see you Crazy Noel" he smiles and acknowledges Jimmy. "You made it through the road block" "Yeah, no dramas", I replied. He hands me the walkie talkie and says "Follow me!" My eyes drift to the fence line and all I see is red dust and a few desperate trees that have been hit with a front-end loader. I turn the stereo down and hear faint music belting off the country side. Scrooge tilts the throttle, the Harley roars as he kicks it into second and raises the front wheel. The car is covered in a barrage of red dust, dirt and gravel. I know Harley's and dirt tracks don't mix but Jimmy belts out, "Fucken love it!" I hit the gas and the car starts slipping and sliding. Scrooge hits on of the corners so hard, that I see through the dust that his elbow is just barely missing the gravel. Jimmy yells," Don't let him get away!" I give him a quick elbow and he starts punching the dash. "You wouldn't be dead for quid's!" Jim replies. "Not if I hit one of those gumtrees, so don't talk too soon." We arrive at the reinforced gate and I see the security, Scrooge leaves his Harley idling, "You right Noel?" "Yeah, no dramas mate, thanks for the escorted short cut." He lowers his shades and says, "Thanks for helping me out that night at Gobbles" "No Worries" I nod and shake his heavily callused hand full of Tattoos. We drive through the gate and I park the car back to front for easy exit access. The February heat smacks us right on the side of the head and the flies stick to you like glue. I say to Jim, don't swallow one of them it's a long way to the hospital. I leave Jimmy back stage and hear his ritual ibuki breathing and screaming at the top of his lungs. I proceed to the entrance and meet with the rest of the band. They gather around as I quickly go down the list. "Don't wander off there are all types of deadly snakes in every colour of the rainbow, check the toilet seat for red back spiders because if you get bitten the hospital is in Perth so you'll probably die in Bindoon." They are used to my Steve Irwin take on the bush, but still listen intently. I don't mention the drop bear (koala bear) story of how they can fall out of the tree and scratch your eyes out we've told that one to all the Canadians and Americans before. The sun sets and as usual, Jimmy rips it up with a scorching set. I can't help but think the ride through got him amped. I make it a point to catch up with Fast Eddie, he suggests we catch up for a ride soon. I sort the travel pack of vodka, lemonade and limes. Jimmy cranks the stereo to full bore, the air-con to freezing point and we hit the road. It's a long drive, but I can only think about the comfort of a hotel room. I forget my earplugs and will just have to settle for Jim's 54 head butt's hoping he'll choke on a lime.

## Divinyls in Bindoon

On another road trip to Bindoon, Rod and I drove Chrissy Amphlett and Mark McEntee from the Divinyls. They spoke about how humiliating some of the shows were in America. When they did support for Aerosmith, the promoters would bring a net down in front of stage as protection from any bottles or objects thrown at them by the fans. Jimmy told me he was in L.A. playing pool with Chrissy against some Mexican gang members. He whispered in her ear, "if you want to get out of here, stop winning" Chrissy's response was "Fuck em" I suppose it was her way of getting back at him for all those times she was the opening act for Jimmy and the fans would chant out Barnesy! Barnesy! Barnesy! Chrissy would go off, while Jimmy giggled back stage. In the early 80's Noel Rush worked as their security/ tour manager. He told me the constant arguments that Chrissy and Mark would endure. However, I found them to be quite funny and entertaining. About an hour into the trip Mark says to pull over he needs to take a leak. "Wouldn't it be funny if you got bitten by a snake Mark?" laughs Chrissy. She starts teasing him about his rock star pants. He proceeds with his business on the side of the road when I notice his leather pants has a zipper that goes from front to back. "You'll fit right in at Bindoon mate, lots of leather jackets there." Then he responds, "Noel can you help me zip up my rear end?" "No fucken way, I should leave you out here for the dingoes to feast." What about you Rod? As Chrissy zips him up, she says Rod and Noel are karate killers, maybe I'll let them loose on you, Mark." They entertained us not only at Bindoon, but on both sides of the road trip.

## Where do I Stand?

The river was high in Bundaberg, a town about 4 hours' drive up north from Brisbane. When you drive past this river at night, you can sometimes catch a glimpse of the red-eye of the crocodile. It was not only known for these dangerous creatures, but prone to flooding. I drive Jimmy and I back to the hotel and wonder if the river banks would burst tonight. It's 3 am in the morning, absolutely pissing down and I'm getting home from the gig. The workers from the iconic Bundaberg Rum or Ginger beer factory are probably beginning their shift. I close my eyes to catch a few moments of rest when the hotel phone rings. "Noel, its Rod mate." He tells me about the restructuring of Zen Do Kai. "We have to reward some of the guys in the club who have opened up more schools." He explains the hierarchy has changed slightly and basically some of my students, people who I trained were given higher ranks. Fazed, confused and a bit surprised I felt a bit gutted. My thoughts quickly turn to disbelief especially as I think about lining up in the honbu. "Where do I stand?" I thought. As if I wasn't doing enough to lift the profile of Zen Do Kai by pushing

Jimmy to train. I suppose touring around the country using Zen Do Kai security at most of the concerts venues wasn't enough. It wasn't the same as opening up schools in Perth. Perhaps standing on the door for 12 hours being abused, getting assault charges and trying to enforce the club style still wasn't enough. All the loyalty from fighting those court cases dissolved and was replaced by feelings of total disbelief. "Oh yeah, and by the way, Dean is going to take over your part in the security equation of the nightclubs in Perth." It's a basic equation. No worries, I realize when someone has been made redundant. However, I've always believed that being made redundant meant that your position is no longer available in the organization, not that you're being replaced. People used to say I had a sense of humour before all of this and depending on how many drinks I've had it's taken about 10 years to get over it. That's a long time for anyone to carry that hostility and resentment. It's like a disease that eats away until it kills you if you let it.

Next morning, I tell Jimmy about the new structuring and he says it was similar to when he left Cold Chisel and went solo. "You just fight like hell to start again." I am no longer bitter towards anyone and although I may have taken a different path I still believe loyalty is valuable and can never be taken away. However, I never stepped back into the dojo again.

## The Rock Pile

On the drive into work at the Racquet Club, I used to say "Just another night on the rock pile, cracking rocks." The burden of the uncertainty was starting to wane as the thought of making money for someone else while collecting enemies along the way. This was why I refused to be a licensee. You take all the responsibility for overcrowding including the criminal charge. Nightclubs are unpredictable, one week a patron is your friend and the next week he can turn on you like a raging bush fire. I was unable to do the 6pm-6am shifts and knew this was my last bouncing gig. I guess when one door closes, another one opens and I was given this opportunity after Michael Brown parted ways with Bob Maher he offered me a position to run the door at the Racquet Club. We had a good working partnership and as a nightclub owner, he took other approaches. He incorporated businesses to have private functions and cocktail parties to cater for the 9-5 crowd. This expanded his mix of patrons while simultaneously making money when the majority of nightclubs were still setting up. Therefore, the Racquet Club attracted suits, footy players, lonely hearts and the CIB, who hung around longer than most. Generally, I didn't mind this crowd, pretty harmless except for the girls who can get feisty after a few too many. Brownie also knew that if Eddie and six coffin cheaters rock up to say hello, I would never refuse them entry due to dress code. It is similar to my mate JK, when he was not allowed to enter any licensed premise that law was out the door with me. Even though, I thought it was not my scene at least it was not as heavy Gobbles. I became friends with Jamal, the owner of the takeaway shop next door, an oil rigger from Dubai who wore his welcome out in his own country. He was not much taller than Tina, about 5' 2 so I told him if he ever got hassled he could always count on me. He was quick to pull out a .45 calibre and said if I was ever in any strife we could count on him.

At this stage of a doorman's life it is like being a boxer, after too many punches in the head, there comes a time to get out. As they say, you are only as good as your last fight. I start to get wind of a rumour that perhaps I'm slipping. The guys who are working with me are a mixed bunch. Julian Kovacs, heavy-set Hungarian, who is studying to become an accountant, convinces me every week not to leave. I'm sure he can read it all over my face. Like Julian, the 'Melon Heads' brothers Shaun and Terry Keating, staunch with good hearts convince me to stick with it. I park my dilapidated *ute* (truck) which has been kicked, vomited on and seen many relationships ruined in the nightclub parking lots. When I arrive, Julian quickly gives everyone the once over. "Heads up guys, get you're back up against the wall" Although, we hadn't had many violent brawls at the Racquet Club, you could never let your guard down. Everyone working in the industry kept tabs on everyone. If there were a group of guys that got kicked out of one nightclub, all the other clubs would be alerted. Basically, we were keeping the wolves at bay. It is near to closing time the night seemed pretty smooth so I leave for a drink and touch base with Rod at EXIT nightclub. I get called back at 2 am regarding Chrissy, the licensee who is having trouble with the same Asian guy who came in last week. We wanted to kick him out but John White, who I've known for 20 years, calmed him down. I'm not against coming to a nightclub with bodyguards. But if you bring them so you can play up, you're a wanker. I could read him straight away and wanted to belt the shit out of him but held back because of John.

Julian has the anxious look as I arrive, I could smell it. He quickly informs me that Mr Chop Suey, wearing a custom made white suit, drinking expensive bottles of champagne and mouthing off has two new bodyguards. Troy Mercanti is one of them who we all knew from working around the traps. He grabbed Chrissy and pulled her down the stairs. Generally, there is a code while working doors, try not to fuck up at another club. He also trained with one of my students, Lance Chipchase and I remember having a brief conversation only a couple of weeks ago. As I walk over to confront them, immediately I sense trouble. The fire in my solarplex starts to ignite when I see him clench the bottle in his right hand. He turns his jaw up and locks eyes with me and gives me the "no response" look. I have seen this particular look so many times before. I see Mr Chop Suey and he glares at me with the same look, "yeah I got my boys to back me up." However, Troy's look is even more compelling as if he didn't recognize me, oblivious, total disregard. This is the ultimate 5 second stare down. So I ask him, "You got a problem with me?" He steps forward and lifts his hand up with the bottle. I wasn't giving him the benefit of the doubt. I step to the side with an over hand right. We start mixing a few blows and he bangs me a few times when Mr Chop Suey distracts me. Julian is keeping the other body-builder looking bodyguard off me. In the midst of chaos, one of the girls on the door lets off some pepper spray. This rattles a few of the boys as I see Jaime head towards the door. I spin around and still see Mr Chop Suey so I hit him with a palm heel and he literally does a mickey flip back. I make sure he is out cold, one for thinking he can mouth off and get away with it and two for being a wanker. I turn to the other bodyguard and give him a hook to match his size. Surprisingly, he lunges back, throws his hands up in defeat and doesn't want to know about it. I see Troy on all fours heading for the door and in disgust I yell out, "Finish him off! Finish him off!" I am in total disbelief as I recall what happened. Troy turned on me and did we do our best? Knowing that we may have to face consequences for our actions, I still have the voice in my head. Take no prisoners, don't give them the benefit of the doubt and don't let go for fuck sake! My reaction always turns to judgement. Did anyone hold back? Was it the pepper spray? Mr Chop Suey threatened to charge us on the way to the hospital. I was thinking about bigger things like retaliation.

This altercation quickly filters through the other clubs like wild fire. Rumours that Troy was seen shooting off his pistol throughout Northbridge. I turn to Jamal, "we may need you tonight, mate." Everyone knows when you are working doors it never ends there. We all head to Aqua bar, a late night club that stayed opened till 6am. I figure if Troy wants to get me he knows where I am. Sometimes things are predictable and like clockwork he shows up with a few of his crew. Rod, Habby and I spill onto the street as the weary-eyed crowd gathers to watch it all go down. It's 5 am and a bit chilly in the air, but my fire starts to ignite again. Do we all jump in like a pack of wolves, for everyone else's pleasure to watch a violent brawl? I look at everyone around and we all know each other. I'm thinking we are all basically in the same boat. I tried reasoning with everybody. At the end of the day, we were all taken back by what happened back at the

Racquet Club, but what were we fighting over anyway? Mr Chop Suey playing up and eventually we are all turning on each other? "Fuck that" I said. Troy seemed evasive, like he was coming to his senses. Moment by moment we all realize that there were never any winners. So we left it at that; backed up and parted ways. A minute ago, it looked like it would have been on for young and old. Perhaps in the light of day, it was like being in a fish bowl. Everyone would see everything, and no doubt it would have been one ugly scene.

Rod was usually the first one to come over on Monday morning for a *cuppa* (cup of tea). We have discussed so many things over the humble cup of tea. The first call I receive on the answering machine is from Troy, in a soft slow voice, "Noel, its Troy...I'm sorry...give me a call back." I give him ten points for the decency to even call. We both said we copped a few lumps and bumps; don't hold a grudge and we'll catch up for a drink. Sometimes I wish some of the other blues I've been in could be solved this way.

One New Year's eve, I ended up at the Aqua bar. There was an altercation between a mate, Andy and some guy who king hit Terry, one of my guys on the door a couple of weeks ago. A violent altercation spilled out onto the street where a guy's finger was bitten off. I remember asking myself the same question; what am I doing here trying to find a cup of ice so we can give the police the rest of his finger.

Michael Brown was opening up another nightclub called Lladro and offered me to run the security for both of his clubs. The more I thought about it, the less I wanted to do it. I knew it was a job, but I no longer wanted to deal with this environment and lifestyle. I was exhausted of people, their misfortunes and the whole security scene. I finished working for Brownie and never worked in another nightclub ever again. I knew at this stage, I was on my own.

# CHAPTER 7

# Rolling around the Circle of Revenge

In the era of plaid pants, feathered fringes and chili con carne life was a struggle. Working for scraps at the Nollamara Hotel with the sound of 'number 21 your chicken schnitzel is ready' and dealing with the two pot screamer wanting to fight everyone in the front bar. He is usually a clone of his parents and has taken over where they have left off. It is Sunday lunch where you just came off the Saturday night graveyard shift. You feel like shit but they can't get any other doorman to stop the anarchy. You deal with the ones that drink a gallon of rum, take their shirt off and call you outside for a flogging. The owners would try and save money by employing one doorman and word would quickly spread through the local that it's easy pickings. I think the owners have seen one too many Bruce Lee movies. In the early 90's the nightclub owners were faced with the compliance of security cameras. It could be your best friend or your worst enemy. The tapes would be reviewed and they would let you know whether they will charge you or not. I know we weren't perfect, but it was not always the doorman's fault. I believe there are three sides to the story, right, wrong and the truth. Shortly after the cameras came in, everyone working in the security industry had to be registered with a number. This eliminated anybody with a criminal record and therefore experienced guys that had one or two convictions. This resulted in popcorn bouncers from Hoyts theatre and parking attendants with black ties and white shirts. You throw them on the door with a clipboard and a couple of models to stamp wrists and within a few weeks the phone would be ringing off the hook. "Can you help us?, we'll pay whatever you want" I've seen it so many times before they spend millions on the fit out but save a few bucks on the public relations or security. This is where I always saw areas of opportunity. You definitely need people to know how to run the room and set the tone. I also learned from the businesses that succeeded by doing the simple things and knowing their market and customer. Rod and I earned the reputation from following no one. We knew how to attract more students. Bob taught us that martial arts were not just for a few tough guy street fighters it was for everybody. Even though we got harassed and had all of our posters around the suburb, at the end of the day we were teaching people a gift of self-awareness and personal development. I told Rod we might as well hang up 'Most Wanted' posters. I suppose we were our own worst enemies. I was driving around in an old Chevy impala with a Mohawk thinking, are you looking at me? Of course, they probably were. We followed through with building up the Perth dojos as a sort of culture branding, similar to what Rock and Roll bands, Motorcycle clubs, Restaurants and

Fashion labels do. The police saw a crew of hard men letting loose on society creating anarchy. This is one of the reasons why they flipped up our place twice too many times hoping to find illegal drugs. On my daily runs to the dojo the local CIB would stop me for an interview which started out something like this, "Where were you on the night Joe Blow got snotted?" I replied, "How the hell should I know?" Then they would say, "Jump in we'll give you a lift." But these days, I was a lot smarter. "No thanks, I'll meet you at the dojo house." They knew they couldn't just bundle me in the car without probable cause. They didn't call me Mr Brash for nothing so as usual I ran in the other direction. After a while Rod complained, that we were getting harassed particularly by this one officer. He was investigated and they found out he was up to no good.

## The Inner Circle

In my inner circle of friends and trusted soldiers there was a black cat. I knew him for over 20 years and was his Sensei. I don't blame any of my misfortunes on him but I learned that if you try to use yesterday's solutions to solve tomorrow's problems it doesn't always work in this type of lifestyle. I visualized it all happening, my sixth sense was telling me Karma was acting up. My actions were being compromised and my closest allies suddenly transformed into enemies. Don't go into battle with an unconscious mind because that's when you end up with a concrete sandwich. In life everyone is a Shogun they surround themselves with loyal allies. In the Shogun circle, eight specialized people fill the inner circle; they are exceptionally skilled and knowledgeable in that position. That person portrays that position by his/her thoughts, actions and mannerisms. These eight positions are the ones of trust as they are protecting the triangle where the Daimyo's and the Shogun sit. These eight positions around the circle are Etiquette, Self-control, Benevolence, Truth, Loyalty, Honour, Justice and Courage. The circle represents karma, the notion that what goes around comes around (or that one's actions will be returned at least twice over) However, when the black cat visits but sits on both sides of the fence you can never relax and let your guard down. Things can quickly change when you drink poison and become infected. Maybe I created the monster as a way of splitting ties with the past and pushing into the future. I missed the link of awareness or the gap in between and more importantly, staying present and focused. I kept hearing about these new associates of the black cat bullying some of the non-threatening type of Zen Do Kai guys. They were simply part-time gangsters wanting all the jelly beans. At the same time these new associates were letting it be known around the nightclub circle that they were the crew you don't want to mess with. Stand over merchants intimidating anyone to increase and heighten their ego and image. The black cat sat on the edge of the circle adding more fuel to the fire. I could no longer surround myself with this environment. I also knew I was never one to walk around like a zombie and let it happen in front of me. I had to look for my own answers in life. I had to realize that life is meant to progress. The doors were closed and only a sliver of light came from underneath. However, this sliver of light was enough to want to change lifestyles and turn off the tap. Besides, revenge is only going to get someone maimed and/or killed. Overtime, everyone gets there Karma, sometimes twice harder. In fact, the black cat and his make believe associate ended up with a double concrete sandwich with gravy all over and I wasn't the cook.

This lesson in karma has brought me more opportunities in life than I could ever imagine. Sometimes I would find inspiration in the most unlikely places. In the Rock and Roll business, travel was high on the agenda which boxes things in perspective. When you meet people and hear their story, you humble yourself and are reminded to be grateful for what you have. I'd do a reality check and think back to working with Grot and Snot laying pipes in the trenches or jackhammering manholes at Wacol in 40 degree heat. How I thought I would be trapped here in this life and that's that. Nothing beats looking up 30 feet to a small hole with the sight of Grot and Snot. Snot being the handsome brother only because he didn't get so drunk one night that his mates tattooed a swastika sign on his forehead. Grot even tried to sand paper it off. They thought they were doing the right thing by using a tea towel to block the sun out. "Are you feeling any cooler Noel?" They'd taunt and haunt me that Wacol jail was only a hop, skip and jump away. I also thought about the drug dealers doing their thing driving in fancy cars with fancy clothes living the fancy lifestyle. Meanwhile as the jealousy fades, I am building my core 'hara' and they are wasting away. The hard labour jobs were a devil in disguise. When I was younger I thought I was cheated because I never had any of that. I nearly joined Grot and Snot in their motorcycle club and became a full-time biker. However, deep down inside I was not only paranoid about being involved in criminal activity but I had to have at least two showers a day. No doubt I would have woken up with a swastika sign as well. When I left Perth, from Brisbane although I aligned myself with another gang of sorts I was always conscious of the working class people. I'd sit in the front seat with the limo driver and form lifelong friendships or hang with the truck driver and crew guys backstage where they made things happen. Similar to martial arts when you reach black belt you don't walk the same, your posture changes and your breathing is more fluid. You also tend to look for opportunity and strive to get out of the rut. I knew I would never work in a 9-5 corporate gig or work in an office environment constantly looking over your shoulder. I found teaching came very easily to me and enjoyed seeing people grow with my help and expand their personal awareness and self-defence abilities. Meanwhile, I was ultimately learning off of my students. One of my students from Adelaide said you have to listen to this band Cold Chisel. It was not long after that I was picking them up from the airport and taking Jimmy to pubs and nightclubs.

## Triggers

I suppose everybody wakes up with triggers. Alcoholics may feel the urge just walking past the pub. Drug addicts can taste one more sniff. It is the craving for a response to your bodies stress distraction. You feel overwhelmed or distracted and there is a tendency to escape. I admit I find it very hard to forgive people if I believe they have done the wrong thing by me. I know it is the poisonous thoughts that reoccur from time to time. I have had this trigger for years it is the part of the brain where you are stuck in the fight or flight response. When I speak to some of the Bushido Brothers today, we still have that same feeling lurking behind us. The atmosphere in a crowded pub sends sparks of nerve energies tingling behind our neck. It is different to have a confrontation these days with mobile phones and surveillance cameras everywhere. We all know the streets have changed, we've changed. I'm sitting on the deck with Gary Pettersen, who worked alongside me on some of Jimmy's tours. We didn't have to say a word, no signals, no verbal conversation; we just knew what each other was thinking. Today we talk about the use-by-date, like a carton of milk. Do we taste it to see if it has gone off? It tastes just as sour as when you're told you are not needed anymore. Unfortunately, for Gary it can be disappointing when the phone stops ringing and promoters turn their back. One day you are making money and then before you know it, nothing. He tells me of his bad day in the park. We all have them, but for Gary it is like wearing a BSA leather jacket in a gay bar. He always seems to attract some kind of outlandish altercation. To clear his head it is six-pack of beer and a walk to the Botanical Gardens. He is approached by 3 young hoons. They pull a knife on him and ask him for all his money. However, even if he defends himself, he may suffer the consequences of knowing how his next punch could be lethal. At times it is better to turn off the tap of revenge because a man who studies revenge keeps his own wounds open, unhealed.

## Go to Hawaii, you'll love it there

I could see the Royal Palace from the hotel room in Kensington. I was waiting for Jimmy to take him to the casino. He handed me an around the world ticket and said "Go to Hawaii, you'll love it there." I never once thought that one day I would end up living here. I remember seeing the old Elvis Presley movies as a kid and thought this place is magical, probably not even real. We got into the lift with one of the security from the Brixton Academy. He tells us he's been shot six times. So I say, "Don't stand next to me then, cause at this point I'm feeling pretty lucky, but you see my mate over there, you can stand close to him" We still had one more gig to do in Brixton which was run by the Rasta's. This is a notorious place and we are all cautious about whether or not this gig will go off drama free. Luckily, Jimmy packs the venue with many of the ex-pats from Australia. It was funny to see some familiar fans in the front row. Tony Brock took me to these underground pubs around London, where we drank warm beer and he tells me all the Rod Stewart stories. The band once filled Rod Stewart's entire hotel room with live chickens. Luckily, I was only a witness to the many, many pranks that the crew were up to. If you fell asleep wasted, you could quite easily wake up the next day painted green. We could never be 'punked' none of that shit ever. I may have a sense of humour, but they knew I would kill them. Whilst in London, I caught up with another Zen Do Kai mate Tony Quinn. He showed me around London, introduced me to Dave Stewart and took me to Annie Lennox's place. Even Tony knew that touring gigs don't last forever. Job security is high on the agenda even if you are the security. One of my favourite perks of travelling was trying the different foods in each country. I would especially pay attention to the street food; and found it so intriguing that you could get good quality food served to you for very cheap from a vendor on the street. It was these experiences with food around the world that sparked my dream of a restaurant. I also began to think about how I was going to go traveling on my own and to not have to worry about ear plugs, 25 pieces of luggage and the vodka travel pack. When I landed in L.A. my bags mistakenly went straight through to Honolulu. It was June of 1988, the sky is clear blue, the sun is bright, there are hotels everywhere and I am dressed in road gear; a Eurogliders 'Groove' t-shirt, jeans and rockabilly Doc Martens. I wander down the street from my hotel, cross the bridge and while I am walking this American guy in black pants and a white dress shirt strikes up a conversation with me. "Where are you going?" he says "No place in particular" I answer thinking 'Is he just being friendly or is he a *mahu* (Hawaiian for gay) trying to make a pass at me?' He is a carpenter from Boston and says he is going to the Hard Rock Café and would I like to join him? I like this place, INXS have a financial interest in the Hard Rock in Sydney. I meet Tina who is born and raised in Hawaii and graduated from college in Philadelphia. She majored in Textiles and was always a creative person drawn to bright colours and patterns. She is intrigued to learn more about Australia and I hope I can make her an offer she can't refuse. When we met she was working for a surf company called Hawaiian Island Creations and fashion retailer Esprit de Corp. We eventually married in Australia where she continued to work in the retail industry until we began to move on (our shared dream of) the restaurant. Building upon our now joint vision, we drew on the backs of napkins and planned for the future.

Caption: Cat, Hulala Breakfast pastries

# Hulala Breakfast

**Fresh Juice of the day**     **high in beta-carotene**     5.50
*Orange Carrot & Papaya*

**Hulala Splash**     **very refreshing**     3.95
*Orange pineapple guava lychee mineral water lime & mint*

**Polynesian Fruit Salad**     **tropical high**     5.50
*Seasonal melons with coconut dressing*

**House Muesli w/ banana & yogurt**     **high in fiber**     6.95
*Packed with oats bran puffed rice coconut dried fruit nuts & more*

**"Puka-Puka" Pancakes**     **hawaiian waffles**     8.95
*Puka or holes in a pancake with house made strawberry syrup & bacon*

**French Toast**     **Classic with a twist**     8.95
*with macadamian-nut golden syrup sliced bananas & bacon*

**"Wiki-Wiki" Breakfast**     **hawaiian time**     9.95
*Two Eggs Bacon Grilled tomato Roasted mushrooms & Hulala toast*

**"Loco-Moco"**     **Local- style breakfast**     9.95
*One egg over our house-made beef patty & Hulala fried rice*

**Smoked Salmon & Dill Scrambled eggs**     10.95
*served with grilled roma tomatoes & Hulala toast*

**Big Kahuna Breakfast**     **When your hungry**     12.95
*Two eggs Bacon oven roasted tomato roasted mushrooms country fried potatoes & hulala fried rice or Toast*

**Assorted phillipine breads & pastries**     **made fresh daily**
*a selection of ensamadas, hopia, an-pan & spanish bread*

**House-made banana & macadamian nut bread**     2.95

## Simply Toasted

| | | |
|---|---|---|
| *The Honolulu* | *Ham Cheese & Tomato* | 4.50 |
| *Tropical Itch* | *Bacon Banana & Cheese* | 4.95 |
| *Maui Wowie-* | *Bacon Tomato Avocado & Cheese* | 5.95 |

## Eggstras     Coffee,tea or else

| | | |
|---|---|---|
| *Egg* 1.50 | *Cafe latte Cappucino Flat white* | 3.00 |
| *Bacon* 1.95 | *Long Black Machiato* | 2.80 |
| *Mushrooms* 1.95 | *Hot Mocha* 2.80    *Short Black* | 2.50 |
| *Country potatoes* 1.95 | *Iced Coffee* 4.20   *Iced Chocolate* | 4.00 |
| *Grilled Tomatoe* 1.40 | *Iced tea* 2.50    *Hot Tea* | 2.20 |
| *Fried Rice* 1.95 | *Orange Tomato Guava & Pineapple* | 3.50 |

*Hulala Breakfast Menu*

*Cat, Yvonne and Tina, Cairns Pupu Platter*

# Food review: Hulala
## HOME MADE HAWAIIN

Looking for something a little bit different to the usual fare? How about Hawaiin cuisine? While the Cairns market covers just about every dining style imaginable, from Korean to Vietnamese, Japanese to Lebanese, etc. etc., Hulala is offering something alternative. Known as 'Pacific Rim Cuisine', the fare is a blend of tastes from Hawaii and round the Pacific that provides some different options for jaded palates.

This cute little café, situated at 45 Spence Street in premises that Café Cyclone and more recently Flavours occupied, is vividly decorated in limegreen and blue with framed pictures of Hawaiian style ads for pineapples etc. Hulala's owner/chef is herself Hawaiian born and most eager to discuss the food of her homeland and the influences and inspirations for the cuisine presented. This is fun style dining — very informal and relaxed with take-out being available on all dishes.

The lunch time menu should be extremely popular as it really is a bit different. Burgers available include Teriyaki Cheese Burger Deluxe ($5.95) with lettuce, tomato and house made mayo; Barbecue Chicken Burger ($6.95), Fishburger or fish taco wraps ($6.95). All breadcrumbed dishes use the light Japanese panko breadcrumbs for fresher flavour. The fish taco wrap comes with Asian mixed slaw and lime mayo in a tortilla and is delicious. Panini triangles are available with different fillings: lemon grass chicken, lemongrass tofu, bacon lettuce & tomato and our favourite, tuna & egg salad with special Hulala mix salad and sprouts. These can also be toasted.

Hulala offers small or large plates of different dishes, all served with rice and salad. The small plates are a delicious lunch and include Huli-Huli Chicken pieces marinated in Hawaiian BBQ sauce ($5.95/$11.95); Korean "kal-bi" Beef Satays mari-nated in sesame soy. These are moist and very tasty with a sweetish flavour to the sauce. Pork Cutlet in panko breadcrumbs with oriental tomato sauce; and Marinated Lamb Cutlets with a rosemary and serrano chilli aioli are also on offer. The Hulala mixed plate covers a selection of these plus a Spring Roll ($9.95/$14.95). This is a great way to sample a range of their dishes. At dinner the Pacific Rim Tapas sampler includes all of these plus house made chilli bean frijole, bean sprout salad, rice and mixed salad, plus three cheese bread. The special touch at Hulala is that everything is made in house, including all the sauces for dipping, mayos, aioli, frijole and chunky chilli spiced version and guacamole with chopped peppers and big chunks of avocado.

The blackboard menu also includes the cutely named Pupus or small sized dishes. From this we tried sand crab spring rolls with a sweet chilli dipping sauce and cream cheese and macadamia nut wontons. Both were excellent with light crispy pastry and no greasiness at all. The other dish to catch our eye for a future visit is the goat cheese wontons. We also sampled their coconut prawns on skewers with a pineapple chilli salsa. These were tender, moist prawns with a nice coconut crust that sealed in the flavours. Once again that touch of housemade sauces makes all the difference.

The tastiest dish we tried was the Thai Chicken Tortilla ($7.95). This is a large flat bread stuffed with spicy Thai chicken heated through and served with guacamole and sour cream. A sort of Mexican-Asian hybrid — definitely Pacific Rim. Vietnamese rice paper rolls are another delicious pupu. We tried one stuffed with coriander rice vermicelli and lemongrass chicken — a very large serve for $3.50. All dishes come with a deli-cious side salad with an unusual dressing of lime sesame and soy that really works beautifully with the Asian flavours.

Desserts are a knock-out option at Hulala. Chocolate Lava Mudflow is based on a Bailey's mousse with homemade icecream. There is a mango mousse, chocolate chewy macadamia brownies, a great sticky toffee pudding, housemade cinnamon and coconut ice-creams. Coffee is well made. - *The Salsa Sisters*

*Cairns Hulala Review*

*Cairns Friends and Regulars*

*Cairns Japanese Tourist and Regular Customers*

# Hulala Cafe & Lounge

**Juice of the Day** a healthy start                                    see specials board

**Yam Cushions** layers of sweet potato, bok choy & mushroom in a puff pastry pillow served w/ sweet chilli plum dip                                                                                        7.95

**Sand-crab Spring Rolls & Goat cheese Wontons** served on hulala slaw with sweet chilli & rosemary serrano aioli (2 serves of each)                                                7.95

**Quesadilla of the Day** 2 large flour tortillas w/ melted cheese & daily fillings served w/ sour cream & house-made guacamole                                              see specials board

**Vietnamese Summer Rolls** fresh rice paper rolls filled with a rainbow of ingredients served w/ nouc cham dipping sauce    please see specials board    2 for 6.95    3 for 8.95

**Vegetarian Lumpia** vege spring rolls served with sweet chilli sauce (2)      3.95

**Bowl of Chips**                                                          with lime aioli   2.95

**Cajun Chips**                                                   spicy chips with lime aioli   3.95

## Mini & Large Plates                                              mini/large

**Huli-Huli Chicken**                                                             6.95/12.95
grilled & marinated in hawaiian barbeque sauce served w/ rice & Hulala asian slaw with house dressing

**Korean-style "kal-bi" Beef Satays**                                            6.95/12.95
marinated in a korean barbeque sauce served with bean sprout salad, rice & Hulala asian slaw

**Breaded Pork loin Cutlet**                                                     6.95/12.95
crumbed pork cutlet served with "katsu sauce "rice & Hulala asian slaw with sesame soy vinaigrette

**Malay Chicken**                                                                     13.95
wok-fried chicken in a sweet oyster sauce with oriental vegetables & soft noodles

**Thai-Chicken Tortilla**                                                              8.95
Flour tortilla filled with thai-spiced chicken   asian veg, cheese & salsa served with rice hulala slaw   sour cream &   chunky guacamole

**Vegetable Frijole Enchilada**                                                       7.95
Fresh-made bean mix in a flour tortilla, stacked with vegetables, cheese & salsa served with rice hulala slaw sour cream &  chunky guacamole

**Butterfly-Coconut Prawns**                                                    8.95/14.95
on crispy potato straws & sweet pineapple chili salsa served with Hulala side salad

**Hulala "Surf & Turf" Mixed Plate**                    (big enough for two)       17.95
Korean beef satays   sesame chicken   coconut prawns  asian slaw salad  rice & vegetarian lumpia

## Hulala Pacific rim Tapa's Plate      vegetarian tapa's available
our signature sampler a journey of little bites   great value at 9.95/person   perfect for two   19.95

| | | |
|---|---|---|
| Sand crab spring roll | Goat cheese wontons | Korean beef satays |
| Sesame chicken   Asian slaw salad | Bean sprout salad | Furikake rice |
| Shanghai eggplant dip | Capsicum relish | Marinated mushroom |
| Vegetable frijole bean | Cheese foccacio | Sweet chilli Mayo dips |

45 Spence St.                                                       #4051-7030

---

*Hulala Cairns Lunch Menu*

# Hulala Cafe & Lounge

## Burgers  Wraps  Foccacios
add side chips 1.00 x-tra

**Hulala Chicken Burger** hawaiian barbeque chicken fillet burger lettuce & mayo   6.95
**Fish Burger** panko-breaded with fresh lettuce, asian slaw & lime mayo   6.95
**Teriyaki Cheese Burger Deluxe** house-made quarter pounder marinated in our own
special seasonings topped with fresh lettuce, tomato, cheese & mayo   7.50
**Vegetable Garden Burger** fresh lettuce, tomato, sprouts & mayo   7.50
**Cajun-Chicken Caesar Wrap** chicken tenders  mixed lettuce  caesar dressing   6.95
**Fish Taco Wrap** breaded fish  mixed slaw  lime-mayo  tortilla wrap   6.95
**Lemongrass Chicken Foccacio**   7.50
oriental spiced chicken  lettuce  carrot  cucumber  cilantro  sprouts  & mayo  on a lightly
toasted  sesame seed  foccacio
**Tuna & Egg Salad Foccacio**   5.95
our original mix of tuna  & egg salad with lettuce  sprouts & mayo  on a lightly  toasted  foccacio
**BLT Foccacio** lightly toasted on a sesame seed foccacio   6.95
add guacamole $1.20 extra
**Hippie Foccacio** Tofu  Guacamole  Sprouts  Cilantro  Cucumber  Carrot  & mayo   7.50
all served with Hulala side slaw

## Healthy Salads
mini/ large

**Caesar Salad** cos asian slaw parmesan Spanish onion in our house made dressing   6.95/9.95
with bacon add   1.75
**Sesame Chicken Jungle Salad**   8.95/12.95
crispy marinated chicken  somen noodles asian slaw  &  chinese sesame dressing
**Cajun Chicken Caesar** spiced tenderloins in our creamy dressing   8.95/12.95
**Coconut Prawn Skewers on Caesar**   8.95/14.95
panko-coconut  butterfly prawns  on  our asian style  caesar salad
**Tofu Salad** seasoned tofu  mixed asian greens  somen noodles & house dressing   6.95/9.95
**Hulala asian slaw side salad** mixed lettuce  asian slaw & house dressing   5.95

| Lavazza coffee | tea | juices | softdrinks | milkshakes |
|---|---|---|---|---|
| Cafe Latte | 3.00 | | Iced Cappucino | 4.20 |
| Cappuccino | 3.00 | | Iced Chocolate | 4.00 |
| Cafe Mocha | 3.30 | | Iced Tea | 2.50 |
| Flat White | 3.00 | | Orange juice | 3.00 |
| Vienna | 3.00 | | Pineapple | 3.00 |
| Short Black | 2.50 | | Hot Tea | 2.20 |
| Long Black | 2.80 | | Hot Mocha | 2.80 |
| Machiato | 2.80 | | Soft drinks | 2.00 |

45 Spence St.                                    #4051-7030

Cairns Lunch Menu

# Chapter 8

# From Street to Plate

## New Stomping Ground

It was a bittersweet moment, as we drove off across the Nullarbor back to Brisbane. Everything I thought I had built up to at this point was thrown into the pool of uncertainty. However, creativity can sometimes only come from uncertainty and chaos. I knew I no longer wanted to be associated with the boy's club mentality. I sometimes believe I would never be able to pull myself out from the deep, dark cave of memories where I sat everyday alongside Genghis. But even he was gone and I was determined to get out of the rut and break the cycle you can be attached to if you have lived on the wrong side of the tracks. I knew I still had some fight left in me. I was determined to come up with something other than the 'hangis' my Maori mates threw in the backyard, where Rod and I charged for beer and a plate of New Zealand grub. The trouble is we lived so close to the police station that it became increasingly difficult to charge people unknowingly. Coloured mice and cockroach races just weren't cutting it, if we wanted to make some real money.

Hulala café was created from visualization, many conversations and sheer determination. It was a way for me to forget all the dark emptiness I felt in Perth and create something that symbolized all the colors of the senjo. One of the primary martial arts philosophies is that of Karma, or put more simply, "What goes around comes around." It is at this stage of 5th Dan or Masters level that the practitioner realizes the full importance of this statement. Usually the practitioner places himself at the center of the octagon and demonstrates the eight angles of attack and what his defensive stragedy will be. It is at this point he must show understanding of himself actually moving along the eight directions in response to any attempted intrusion upon his physical, psychological or spirtual harmony. Everything you have learned from beginning or white belt is done with containment but at 5th Dan level.

Initially, we thought about moving back to Hawaii to start a small business, but the exchange rate would mean losing 25% of our savings and the timing wasn't right. Sometimes when you are trying to look for a change in life or another environment that may or may not bring you happiness or money, you need to look at your core being first. Your hara or stomach has to be in the right place. We realized you have to be true to yourself and focus on what matters most such as health, well-being and loyalty. Feeling that the time was right for something new, we began assessing our financials and planning for the first step towards the restaurant of our dreams. It was the shared vision of a restaurant that had affordable good quality food, and created an atmosphere that encouraged people to come in for a beer and Pupu's. We could have easily bought a sandwich business near the hospital or a takeaway fish and chip shop and made a stack of cash. However, we weren't chasing material wealth or a magazine review if you invest in advertising dollars. We cared less about that and existed only for the regulars rather than the adventurous foodie waiting for the next culinary delight. We wanted to create a place that was unique and special not franchise cookie cutter. In the restaurant business there are many components. It is ten things or more at once. We preferred to create something that replicated what I saw in the streets of Japan like Nagoya Wings or this famous Izakaya bar where the chefs sit in seiza and serve everything from a wooden paddle. We wanted the feeling of something that was totally unexpected. When people walked in we wanted the ambience to send them to that 'hole in the wall' they enjoyed on some tropical island or last travel place. It all started with developing a concept and site criteria through research. This was hard-core pavement pounding research not worldwide web. We scoured cafes and restaurants to see the different concepts and themes each one presented, figuring out what resonated with us and what wouldn't work. We knew who we wanted to cater to and the kind of vibe we wanted the café to have. Focusing on surf culture and the people who followed that lifestyle; we wanted our restaurant to appeal to those people who would be forever young and connected on a relaxed, casual, "love-life" attitude. The final goal of our vision was the restaurant's location. It all came down to where these people were, and where we knew the restaurant would succeed. Tina was inspired by the food of Hawaii of course, and had her mind set on something which reminded her of home a food truck without the wheels. However, you have to take one step at a time before you realize your dream. This vision was the driving force we used as our business plan, expanding upon it to plan for our future and the restaurant's eventual opening. We believed in this vision, even though we had no restaurant experience in either of our pasts, it was our belief that kept our dreams alive and pushed us to continue to work towards it. This vision brewed in the back of our minds for years, until finally we began to set our plan in motion. Restaurants at the time were very formal and expensive, offering sub-par food at ridiculous prices. People buy restaurants because mistakenly they think they are buying an exciting fashionable lifestyle. Some of them don't realize what they are buying is a potential white elephant that can drag them down and wring all the hope and emotions out of their lives. However, similar to martial arts if you have the focus, attitude and drive you can be successful. However, our lack of experience meant that first and foremost we would need to learn how a restaurant runs and to dive in the deep end of the industry head first. In the mid 90's we purchased a fully established 55-seater BYO pizza, pasta cum blackboard menu. It was in a fairly affluent suburb on the outskirts of Brisbane, Australia. Recognizing our weakness of not knowing anything about the restaurant industry, it was a practical idea for us to start with a restaurant that was already established to learn the basics. While this decision turned out well for us and we were able to use the hands-on knowledge to our advantage it was still a very risky move. It was probably backwards-type insane thinking but we were both crazy anyway. It was probably because we didn't know enough about the industry to see it would have clearly struggled once everyone found out the prior chef had sold leaving behind his cook. By the third month we knew we were knee deep "in the shit." At the same time, the prior owner opened another restaurant and hired back his cook. It was a blessing in disguise which actually did us a favour because we were virtually flying blind. The two week's training did not cover enough for us to succeed on that knowledge alone. Realizing that we needed to make a change fast it was a good decision to bring in a head chef, who had been in the industry for years, knew how a kitchen was supposed to run, and who specialized in the kind of food we wanted to serve. Taking it for what it was, a learning experience, this is where we made most of our mistakes and began to understand what it really took to run a restaurant. Our chef developed a Mediterranean and Asian menu and we incorporated some of our ideas from Hawaii. We changed the menu every six to ten weeks until we found a base menu to work with. We quickly learned the formula for running a kitchen, costs and margins, menu planning, cooking and buying quality ingredients. We were constantly prepping stock levels to meet turnover needs and were aware of the constant fine tuning. Like any new business, we had high hopes. The food industry cooking or being a chef can be difficult, especially for young, passionate and talented chefs. The hours are long and you are constantly on your toes ready to take on the night. Chefs and cooks are working when all their friends are out socializing. It is a stressful sometimes humiliating environment and some rely on alcohol or drugs to get through. I can understand how frustrated chefs get when customers want to come in at 9pm when the kitchen is closed and they are ready to clock out. For me it was a stark reminder of the bulk buying of drinks at the Thornlie hotel with the dreaded countdown. As a karate mentor, I was very aware of getting the best out of people by encouraging rather than criticizing or yelling. However, I had high expectations and standards, so like a ninja; I watched and observed from the sidelines. I had to keep most of what I saw inside, bottled up because this was not the security industry. I knew for the most part I couldn't hold back and therefore I was sometimes faced with my own humiliation. So I let Tina and the chef work their creative magic and I worked in as best I could. Tina absorbed everything too and kept it all in her brain. I learned about all the equipment and how it worked and how to maintain everything so we didn't have to pay for outside labour costs. I added 25-30 extra seating in order to increase revenue. The business part of the restaurant was also very challenging and something we had to learn along the way. But because Tina was the only one that received a proper education and had worked in a business environment in the past, she handled most of the financials. We used all of our own capitol and Julian Kovacs, who was now my accountant stressed the importance of keeping track of all our expenses. I had also not planned to bring any outside investors as this was crucial in our stepping stone ahead of us on the path to Byron Bay. As the menu became increasingly popular the business started to grow and we needed to bring in more staff. However, the menu was too complicated if the chef got sick or needed time off. The chef's menu meant we were meticulous about suppliers, buying Moreton Bay bugs and bringing in fresh tuna and local fish every other day. He brought in a fresh pasta supplier for custom-made tortellini's along with a signature pumpkin and pistachio ravioli. We incorporated gourmet pizza and quesadillas and with the ever changing menu it was also an expensive and time consuming exercise. However, we also wanted the chef to have full rein over what he could create. At one point the chef suggested we do a Sunday Brunch. He was enthusiastic and determined on the Monday a week before the menu came out. However, on the first Sunday opening he showed up with a bad head and our baker with a ton of croissants. Cross out the croissants and he ended up making bread pudding instead. I asked the chef to come up with a simplified Tapa's style menu, so that we could bring in another apprentice chef on his days off. It was based on 12 items and customers could choose any three for a set price. Little by little it was all starting to come together even though this wasn't the restaurant we dreamed of, we used it to the full of its advantage before selling after two years after buying.

After we sold, we moved back to Hawaii for three years so Tina could spend time with her family and I could re-skill myself to pursue our next business venture. We kept saving our money and really narrowing down and focusing our vision. We knew our next stepping stone would be to open up a new café restaurant and test run our concept. This would be our first try at building something from the ground up. We again took all of the lessons from the past, gathered all the information, argued about bento boxes and I attended Bartending school in Hawaii and tried to memorize about 250 cocktails. The hum also returned. I moved back to Australia first to scout locations and decided upon Cairns, Queensland a popular Australian tourist destination known not only for eco-tourism but where the Rainforest meets the Great Barrier Reef. It was Hulala Café part one, our official test run. We wanted to make sure that when we finally opened Hulala Café in Byron Bay, it would be clear to guests that we knew what we were doing. With the high rent and large amount of well-travelled locals and tourists in Byron Bay we wanted to make a strong positive impression when we finally got there. Seeing the danger of going into a business in a tough industry, especially in a place with high rent, we needed the security of knowing that all we would need to focus on was getting customers in the door and not internal issues. We especially wanted to get our menu sorted out and the dishes perfected; this was how Hulala in Cairns really helped. Because the people and town were similar to Byron Bay's; testing out the dishes in Cairns gave us the opportunity to see how they would respond to the culturally diverse dishes.

Now that we were opening up our restaurant from the ground up, we found a café that could easily be transformed. It was easier to find an established place with most of the plant and equipment, rather than start from scratch with an empty shell. We were also aware that we did not want to pay for goodwill either as we were not buying someone else's concept. Knowing that we wanted to create a space that was visually inviting a tropical "tiki-bar" theme, we vividly decorated the walls with wasabi lime green and framed 50's Hawaiian-style ads. We filled the restaurant with novelty Hawaiian memorabilia and hand-painted wine bottles. Tina collected all of her grandmother's blankets, quilts and pillowcases to add that retro feel. She sewed all of the tablecloths and we re-covered the chairs we bought for $2 each at the local lifeline. We believed that no detail was too small and this hand-made vibe made a huge difference in contributing to the atmosphere of the café. While Tina was the mind behind the decorations and colours I used past experience in clubs and bars played a mix of old school and contemporary Hawaiian music. Together we built something totally different than anything that we had come across in our travels and research. Our vision was finally coming to life.

Starting the first Hulala Café in Cairns gave us the opportunity to test our menu and skill set in the kitchen. In the early days, we did Breakfast, Lunch and Dinner. This proved to be suicide, so we concentrated on Breakfast, Lunch and Catering. The catering was a smart move which quickly grew to 25% of sales and allowed us to really utilize our product. We sourced two excellent bakers. An Italian artisan bread maker who made our focaccia's and scotch baps which we used for our Teriyaki-deluxe, Huli-Huli chicken, and Panko-crusted fish burgers. The lunch time menu was extremely popular due to how different it was. We did Lemongrass chicken focaccias and fish taco wraps which proved to be popular with not only the tourist but the locals as well. By chance we aligned ourselves with a Filipino lady, a pastry chef at the Hilton who recently left to start her own bakery business. We brought in ensemada's, hopia, an pans and sweet bread for our French toast. Our full lunch menu even included marinated lamb cutlets, coconut prawns, pork tonkatsu and a fresh catch. We set out perfecting all our dishes on the menu and it was important that we tweaked ingredients to make the dish healthier and appeal to the growing trend of eating consciously.

Knowing that we wanted this menu to eventually be taken to Byron Bay, the menu was a set of small pupu dishes where people could come for a "beer and a bite" Taking the recipes from the Hawaiian style plate lunch (dishes that local people eat on a regular basis, usually a combination of marinated & grilled meat, potato/mac salad, and white rice),local Hawaiian dishes( a medley of Asian-fusion dishes), and some family recipes from Tina's mother we were confident this concept would fit in well with the Byron Bay lifestyle. We began integrating Asian and Mexican tacos and quesadillas which ultimately was the basis of our menu. The most popular signature dish was the Hulala Pupu Platter: A Journey of Little Bites. It was a good dish to share between people, and worked as a way of introducing people to Hawaiian cuisine. Another popular aspect of our menu was that all the sauces, marinades and dressings were house made. Because of the fusions we created in the sauces we offered, it was flavours that some people of Cairns had never experienced before. Because we wanted our dishes to be affordable we knew we couldn't spend a lot of money on expensive ingredients. We focused on fresh, local food that had a reasonable shelf life and could be used in many of our dishes. Due to the nature of a tropical environment the farmer's market in Cairns had some of the best produce in the world.

After a year in Cairns, we felt ready to finally make the move to Byron Bay. We wanted to bring along Sammy

Kano, who owned Yama's Japanese Sushi restaurant next door and incorporate a sushi and sake bar alongside us in Byron Bay. He is the one partner that I would have gone into business with. Although, he made several attempts to sell and move down to Byron, he sponsored many Japanese employees which proved difficult for him to pack everything up and start again. For me, I knew it was a town that was far enough to keep me out of trouble and I liked it because nobody knew me.

Securing a location in Byron Bay after only one week of being there I realized that if you find a place inside that you can re-visit whether they were successes or failures, this ultimately will help determine what opportunities to embrace. Someone was looking after us. I've often found that with all of the decisions I've made in life, I went deep inside to find that feeling. I guess some people call it instinct. When we drove past, it was a bit run down by the previous owner who had an Indian Café for 4 months. It had a license and could fit about 30 people. It was a bit open, but I thought it had potential. I was already building things in my head. We leased a corner space in a commercial building off the main road that runs through Byron Bay. It had a unique feel because it was the only commercial building among residential properties. We were only one of 4 tenants sharing the ground level building with the Iconic East Coast Blues Festival. Our landlord Tony Narracott, was a true Byron identity. His only wish was to see people succeed in business. I think he was happy to see that Hulala became that place for Byron locals to gather before sadly passing away a day after we handed over the café to the new owner in 2007. The transition to Byron Bay was relatively easy. We did little advertising and used the "Taste of Byron" festivals as a marketing exercise. However, a notable difference to our other cafes was that once the restaurant became popular enough, this helped to maintain the level of control over our guests that some restaurants only experience if they are expensive and obnoxiously exclusive. For us the atmosphere was extremely important, and that included our customers. If a customer was rude to our waitresses or caused trouble in the past, they would not be welcomed back. However, Tina made it a point to remember all of our customers by name no matter how few times they may have come in. She wanted Hulala to be a place where customers felt like they were walking into an old friend's home. The vision we believed in for so long had finally come into full bloom and continued to thrive among the Byron Bay local community. The atmosphere we created attracted such a myriad of people it was not long before I met old friends and made new lifelong friends. Steve Fyfield was an old Zen Do Kai mate that lived in the hills above Byron Bay. Like many others who take up residence they come to heal as it is a very spiritual place. In the early days as a teenager in Brisbane, he convinced me not to quit Zen Do Kai when I became disillusioned with the club. His persistence kept me going and I've never forgotten that conversation. When he found out we were opening Hulala, he made it very clear to everyone that Hulala was a "concept" not a "gimmick." He was eager to help me with the business because he cooked lentils in jail and said the boys always came back for seconds. However, when we opened the café in Sept. 2002 unfortunately he was double booked. One of the funniest true story is that he was well known for making some of the best hash cookies in the world. He invited some visiting Mormons in for tea and cookies and they nearly ended up in the hospital. It wasn't determined whether he did time for that but the story went viral across the world. The last time he was thrown in the back of a police car, he pulled his sim card out of his mobile phone, chewed it up into little pieces and swallowed it. Like me and many others who take up residence to find inner peace within to get through their journey in life, it was nice to know Steve was one of the staunchest mates I ever had. If I was on his phone list, I too would have been grateful.

As customers began trickling in news of the restaurant began to spread throughout the community. Even though we were getting some recognition it was Jon Laurenson, owner of Electric Sunglasses that really put us on the map. Walking in one night with some friends and his mum Kerry, he began holding his company parties here whenever he was in town. It also was the local Byron surfing community that began promoting the restaurant's name and reputation. Geoff McCoy, Mieko, Gary and Katie Burmester, Max and Yvonne Pendergrast, The Cooks from Lennox Heads, Roy and Marilyn, Will Conner, Beau Young, all the staff from the surf shops in town and so many staunch supporters who became part of the Hulala Ohana. The waitresses who shared our vision with us like Cat, Gina, Daphne, Sophie, Nicole, Barbara and Tiemi and also helped promote Hulala for us. When the Blues Festival changed direction, I began to see the crew I toured with many years before. We were soon attracting famous musicians, professional surfers and celebrities such as Jack Johnson. Word of mouth was now our strongest and only advertising strategy.

The atmosphere we created drew people in and gave the restaurant character. We basically tried to do everything ourselves which ultimately also took a toll on our overall well-being. Like any idyllic coastal town, Byron Bay had its fair share of attracting problems. We had a sign at the door, "We are a licensed venue, Bottled wine and Good vibes only." I didn't want to turn business away from anybody, but sometimes you get that gut feeling about people. It must be from years of working on the door. I was just trying to make a living, minding my own business and avoiding any confrontations.

Building a business from the ground up, especially in an industry that demands more hours than most, requires 24/7 preparation and execution throughout the year. The restaurant was open from Tuesday to Saturday every week. On Sunday's we would fix anything up that needed repairing in the restaurant and do a thorough cleaning. On Mondays it was catching up with stock levels, shopping and paperwork. There were hardly any days of rest. We didn't want to bring anyone in to alleviate some of our responsibilities. We vacationed once a year to visit Tina's family in Hawaii, and would have to close the restaurant the entire time that we were gone. Hulala was getting busier and busier, but we had not planned to expand. We leased the duplex from our landlord Tony, which was convenient especially when we were running low on alcohol or supplies. However, it was difficult to shut off from everything. Byron Bay was a party town that exploded at the seams at certain times of the year. We felt it was important for our sanity to move to a quieter house about 5 minutes away. It was a typical move for us, throw all of our house belongings in the back of the mini yellow suzuki van (we called the 'butter box') and unpack it all on our next day off. It was a busy Friday night Oct. 7, all the boys from Electric were there for a quiet get together. Both Tina and I were looking forward to the first good nights rest in a long, long time. For us it was just starting to peak before the busy summer season. We were just training up extra staff for this busy time. At about 2 am. in the morning, we are awakened by a pounding on the door. I recognize it, cause it is definitely copper's knock! "A car has run into your kitchen." says the female police officer. This was the second time a car has damaged the restaurant but this time it was serious. So many things are running through my mind as we jump back in the 'butter box' with the clothes we slept in. We see the tow truck trying to pull the ford station wagon through the front of the cafe. It is total devastation, he managed to drive right through the front make shift Gilligan island gates through the point of sale and just past the sliding glass door into the kitchen. All the equipment located towards the front was completed crushed. I call Tony Narracott to tell him about the mess at the cafe. He rushes over and assesses the damage with us, he also knows who the drunk driver is and is friends with his family. Part of his building has been totally smashed into. The drunk driver who not only blew six times over the limit, lost his license for 3 years and was slapped a $200 fine. Fortunately, he didn't kill anyone and we weren't living behind the building. If I found him there after the accident, I can only imagine, what I would have done. I do believe that everything happens for a reason and how creative you get with Karma is up to you. It took 5 weeks to get the restaurant up and running again with new equipment, better security gates and a new and improved Hawaiian-style hut. This gave us the motivation to put the restaurant on the market with a totally new aura. Convinced that the restaurants reputation was enough evidence for an outsider to believe in our concept the way we always had, we hoped we would be able to ask for a good profitable price. The price decided on was meant to set a foundation for our future endeavours and eventual move back to Hawaii. Our intentions were for a strong sale of the restaurant especially after all the hard work and time we put into it. One thing we insisted on throughout the process was to follow the vision not a business plan. We insisted on being driven by the concept of Hulala and not a set of financial goals over time. The key to this was execution and bringing our vision to life. Although the restaurant was really the child we never had, we wanted to sell it as a package and give the new owner a base to work from. We sold the restaurant with good energy and hoped that Hulala would continue. We felt good that we were able to create something and run it with some success. From the struggles of our first BYO, when we had no idea what we were doing. We were able to step back and rather than being blinded by ego or pride, we recognized our weaknesses and made rational decisions on how to improve the situation. We focused on the big picture and how everything played into that, rather than how it was going on a smaller scale. We always knew that each step along the way was a *step*, never letting ourselves get distracted by the little things. Focusing on going in, learning what we needed to learn and moving on. That is what helped us reach our goals. We felt we have come full circle. We taught ourselves how to run a business from a concept that we came up with. I taught myself how to cook and working out the similarities of martial arts. The kata's or choreagraphed moves are similar in running a kitchen. The components like stamina, focus, discipline and peripheral vision all need to be maintained. Similar to a martial arts grading, when you reach black belt it is the start of the journey. You have learned the basics and now you start to develop your own identity.

In this cautionary tale, just remember when your slipping through the stomping ground with your best swagger on, hoping to get what everyone else has, take three deep breaths and let the system set you free. Make peace, not war because you don't have to die by the sword.

*Chimichanga (Tiemi Hatano), Jack Johnson wuz hea, Byron Bay Surf and Tiki Plate*

*Habby Heske, Neil Young, Steven Curry, Geoff McCoy and Mieko*

*Katie and Gary Burmester, The Cooks, Keikis, Nicole and Daphne*

*Hulala Gilligan Island Parties*

# HULALA... HAWAIIAN ASIAN MEXICAN LICENSED CAFE

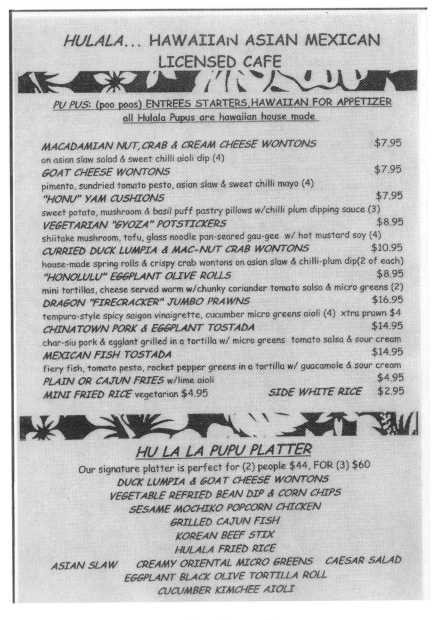

### PU PUS: (poo poos) ENTREES STARTERS, HAWAIIAN FOR APPETIZER
#### all Hulala Pupus are hawaiian house made

**MACADAMIAN NUT, CRAB & CREAM CHEESE WONTONS**      $7.95
on asian slaw salad & sweet chilli aioli dip (4)

**GOAT CHEESE WONTONS**      $7.95
pimento, sundried tomato pesto, asian slaw & sweet chilli mayo (4)

**"HONU" YAM CUSHIONS**      $7.95
sweet potato, mushroom & basil puff pastry pillows w/chilli plum dipping sauce (3)

**VEGETARIAN "GYOZA" POTSTICKERS**      $8.95
shiitake mushroom, tofu, glass noodle pan-seared gau-gee w/ hot mustard soy (4)

**CURRIED DUCK LUMPIA & MAC-NUT CRAB WONTONS**      $10.95
house-made spring rolls & crispy crab wontons on asian slaw & chilli-plum dip(2 of each)

**"HONOLULU" EGGPLANT OLIVE ROLLS**      $8.95
mini tortillas, cheese served warm w/chunky coriander tomato salsa & micro greens (2)

**DRAGON "FIRECRACKER" JUMBO PRAWNS**      $16.95
tempura-style spicy saigon vinaigrette, cucumber micro greens aioli (4)  xtra prawn $4

**CHINATOWN PORK & EGGPLANT TOSTADA**      $14.95
char-siu pork & egglant grilled in a tortilla w/ micro greens  tomato salsa & sour cream

**MEXICAN FISH TOSTADA**      $14.95
fiery fish, tomato pesto, rocket pepper greens in a tortilla w/ guacamole & sour cream

**PLAIN OR CAJUN FRIES** w/lime aioli      $4.95

**MINI FRIED RICE** vegetarian $4.95      **SIDE WHITE RICE**   $2.95

## HU LA LA PUPU PLATTER
Our signature platter is perfect for (2) people $44, FOR (3) $60
DUCK LUMPIA & GOAT CHEESE WONTONS
VEGETABLE REFRIED BEAN DIP & CORN CHIPS
SESAME MOCHIKO POPCORN CHICKEN
GRILLED CAJUN FISH
KOREAN BEEF STIX
HULALA FRIED RICE
ASIAN SLAW    CREAMY ORIENTAL MICRO GREENS    CAESAR SALAD
EGGPLANT BLACK OLIVE TORTILLA ROLL
CUCUMBER KIMCHEE AIOLI

*Byron Bay Dinner Menu*

## HU LA LA GRASS SKIRT SALADS
asian slaw, organic rocket micro greens & crispy cos lettuce

"HULI HULI" HAWAIIAN BBQ CHICKEN SALAD          $15.95
marinated chicken tenders tossed with a creamy oriental aioli dressing
SESAME CHICKEN JUNGLE          $15.95
mochiko popcorn chicken  somen noodles  &  miso-satay sesame soy vinaigrette
BLACKENED CAJUN FISH CAESAR          $15.95
spicy dusted fish  parmesan cheese  red onion  &  house-made caesar dressing
CAJUN PRAWN CAESAR fiery tiger prawns  &  caesar salad dressing  $16.95
HIPPIE TOFU NOODLE SALAD          $14.95
tofu  somen noodle  miso satay  &  sesame soy vinaigrette

## HU LA LA BIG ISLAND PLATES
VEGETARIAN BEAN QUESADILLA          $15.95
 mexi-refried beans, cheese in 2 flour tortillas w/ sour cream, guacamole & asian slaw
THAI CHICKEN QUESADILLA          $16.95
 mild-spiced chicken, cheese in 2 flour tortillas w/ sour cream, guacamole & asian slaw
CAJUN FISH SOFT TACOS          $17.95
grilled fish, lime aioli & mixed slaw with guacamole tomato salsa & corn chips
VEGETABLE FRIJOLE ENCHILADA          $15.95
mexican whipped beans wrapped in a flour tortilla with cheese & salsa served
with sour cream guacamole asian slaw & fried rice box
THAI CHICKEN TORTILLA          $16.95
thai spiced chicken baked in a flour tortilla w/ cheese & salsa served with sour
cream guacamole asian slaw & fried rice box
"MISOYAKI" SATAY BAMBOO CHICKEN STIX          $17.95
marinated in miso & beer chicken tenders & served with fried rice & asian slaw
GRILLED KOREAN "KALBI" BEEF SKEWERS          $17.95
teriyaki stix served with cucumber kimchee aioli salad & fried rice
HULALA HAWAIIAN BAR-BE-QUE PRAWNS          $21.95
caramelized in pineapple bbq sauce with oriental asian salad & fried rice
"SURF & TIKI "MIXED PLATE          $22.95
grilled beef skewers  misoyaki chicken stix  &  barbeque prawns  with vege
fried rice  asian slaw  oriental micro greens  &  caesar salad (2 of each)
"HUMU NUKU" SEAFOOD MIXED PLATE          $22.95
grilled spicy fish  tempura prawns  &  mac-nut crab wontons  with vege fried
rice  asian slaw  oriental greens  &  caesar salad  with firecracker aioli

*Byron Bay Dinner Menu*

177

*Hulala Surf Parties, Malibu Surf Club Ohana*

*Summer Electric Parties, Jon Laurenson, Kong and Mates*

*Hulala Friends, Beau Young Ohana, Gravy and Tiemi*

# ABOUT THE AUTHOR

Noel Watson, a 6th degree black belt grew up street fighting in Brisbane, Queensland. He has operated 3 cafes and a landscape garden business. He lives in Hawaii with his wife and enjoys vintage motorcycles and organic gardening.

*Noel Watson*